AF230098

SEX

&

THE

CHURCH

THE BIOGRAPHY OF KIRK DONALDSON

BY

DON KIRKSEY

CHAPTER 1

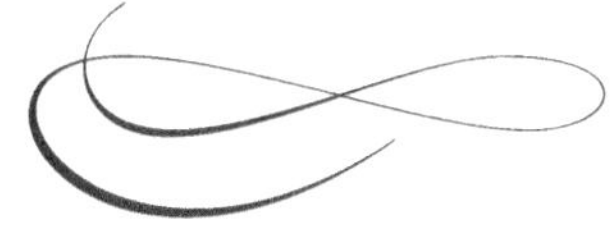

It was a Sunday afternoon. I was laying on the bed in the master bedroom pretending to be sleeping. I could hear her moving out her clothes and other personal belongings. Even though there had been no conversation, I felt it coming. We had separated a few times before when she had gotten involved with men. She always came back; But, This time I knew, she would not be back. When I heard the car start and drive away, I got off the bed and walked down the long hallway to the kitchen, where on the kitchen table was a note addressed to me. It was brief, "I have been in love with someone else for a long time. Take care of my children. Tell them I love them."

I had met Bonnie 16 years before in a college musical. She was the best looking girl in the show, home coming queen, and secretary of the student body. I was about a week late getting into rehearsals. A very friendly guy, named Alvin, helped me get caught up on the music. I noticed he always stood very close to me when helping. After each rehearsal most of the group went to a local pizza restaurant. Most had beer. After some shifting around, I was sitting next to Bonnie. When she looked at me, I could see how beautiful she was. I could overlook the smell of the beer on her breath Just to sit next to her. She asked what I was drinking. I told her, "Root beer."

The next night, I took her to a drive in theatre. A few nights later we went to a party. She seemed to know everyone there. After the party she and I and Alvin and a girl named Helen drove up in Palo Verde, parked and watched the witch in the light house. This was a popular optical illusion. I kissed her for the first time. I noticed in the back seat that Alvin and Helen were doing some heavy necking.

Over the next few months I met Bonnie's parents and her grandmother. They were Christians and seem to quickly accept me.

* * *

When the college year books came out. The students were busy writing greetings. Alvin wrote in mine, "I admire you and Bonnie getting together, the way you have. I wish the same could happen to Helen and me."

I told him, "Alvin, I don't understand." I knew that Helen was fond of him.

He said, "After our next class lets go to the little café by the school and I will explain."

After class, walking to the café, I started thinking, Alvin reminds me of a boy in high school. He and I were walking home from a movie on a dark night when he asked me, "Have you ever had your cook sucked?"

The statement scared me. I said, "No!"

"Would you like to?"

"No, No, No".

Alvin walked in the Café and we got a quiet corner in which to sit.

I looked at him and before he could say anything, I said, "You are homosexual".

"Yes."

"That is hard for me to understand."

"I'll bet it is. As you know, Kirk, I love to dance. I even like to neck and kiss girls: But, The thought of intercourse with a woman makes me sick at my stomach."

"I have never had sexual relations with anyone", I said.

"Well! I couldn't do it myself; But, I have friends that could show you what a great lives we have."

"No thanks. I have had many opportunities to get sexually involved with girls, and I have not. I have had a few opportunities with men also. The reason that I do not is that it is against my Christian principals to have sex outside of marriage."

He replied, "I believe in God. However, I have always been homo sexual so I guess that God made me that way."

"I am not an expert on sex; But, I have a strong feeling that the desire is like having a desire for more money. So if I should rob a bank should I blame God for giving me the desire for more of the things that money can buy? How about killing someone that caused a problem for me. What I am saying is God did not give us the freedom to do anything we want to do."

"You are very hard on gays, comparing us to bank robbers and murderers."

"No. I am not. I oppose any and all punishment of, or prejudice against gays. You say you believe in God. What God? Do you accept Jesus as the Christ? Where do you get your information? That is, information about how to live?"

"I just believe that there must be a God."

"Let me give you just a little reading to do. You do have a Bible at home? I want you to pick it up when you get home from school today and read,   1 John, chapter 1, verses 5 through 10. 'If *we claim to have fellowship with God and continue to walk in a state of ignorance, we lie and do not live by the truth.*' The Bible is the word of God. It is the truth. Every bit of it. That is where I get the information no sex outside of marriage. According to 1 Corinthians, chapter 7, '*But since there is so much immorality, each man should have his own wife.*' Let me suggest that you read *Leviticus Chapter 18, verse 22*, in fact all of *chapter 18* deals with sex." After you do, I want you to tell me if you believe in God or violate His word. There is no in between. You accept or reject. And, you can't accept then start making exceptions".

* * *

Parked in my car in front of Bonnie's grandmother's house, I told her about my conversation with Alvin. She said, "I agree with your attitude toward homo sexual people. However I cannot agree with your attitude toward sex outside of marriage. I had sex with one boy in high school and about a half dozen or so in college. My philosophy on sex is if you like a guy you do it. No one gets hurt. It is very enjoyable. You say you have never had sex?"

"I don't mean to sound like a preacher. Pardon me if I do. Jesus gave his life. It is the least that I can do to give my time a talent. I have been tempted many times. Temptation is not the problem. Everybody faces temptation, even Jesus did. *Matthew, chapter 4, verses 1 thru 11.* How we deal with temptation is what counts. Do we demonstrate that faith in God can shield us from giving in to sin? In the Old Testament, Joseph gave us one way of escape; *Recognize sin as an affront to God and run from it.* Jesus gave another; *Answer temptation with truth from God's Word.* I suggested to Alvin that when he is facing temptation, see it as an opportunity to make God and His word real in his life. You told me that you are a Christian. You no doubt have been told to not just, 'talk the talk', but also, 'walk the walk'. Another way of saying the same thing is 'Don't let your behavior contradict your professed belief'. If our conduct doesn't harmonize with our claimed belief our claim is nullified."

"Kirk, I respect you and I would like to see a lot of you in coming years."

"Will you go to church with me and give the primary intent of your life to belief in and following the word of Jesus Christ ?"

This beautiful woman became my wife four months later.

CHAPTER 2

Bonnie graduated a few months before we were married. I had another year to go for my bachelor's degree. We moved into my little 1200 square feet house in an old neighborhood where the average person was 40 years older than we, and had about a tenth grade education. The train track was 3 houses away, the street was dirt. I worked 4 hours a day and went to school full time. Bonnie was fine for the first few months. Then she complained about her life situation, I would tell her how fortunate we were to live in a house that was paid for compared to her friends that rented apartments. At the time I had no appreciation for the big adjustment she had from a very gregarious college life.

"I want a dog."

I said, "What kind of dog?"

"Any kind of dog. Just a dog to keep me from going out of my mind alone here by myself, 13 hours a day."

"OK, tomorrow we will go to the county animal rescue center and get a dog for you."

She picked out a mixed breed, medium size dog. Every day for the first two weeks the dog wet or pooped in the house.

"Kirk, I have tried and tried. I take him out, walk him, and bring him back in and he messes in the house almost immediately."

We got rid of the dog.

Every Sunday after church we went to her mother's or my mother's house for dinner. One Sunday her mother commented about that beautiful dog and how playful he was. This surprised me because Bonnie had never mentioned her mother visiting. This should have tipped me off about things to come. Why did she not mention that her mother had visited while I was at work?

* * *

Pastor R S Parker stopped us leaving church and asked if we could stay a few minutes. We went to his office. "I am happy that you two are regulars at services. I have a favor to ask of you. The leader of the teen age group moved away and I want you two to replace her."

"Wait a minute. We are just out of our teens ourselves. Don't you need a more mature couple?"

"No. More mature is too old to identify with those in the group."

"Will you give us a few days to think about it?"

"Yes. This is a very important job. And I believe you two could do it well."

We thought about it and talked about it for a few days. I explained to Bonnie that she would have to carry most of the load because school, and my job. She made the call.

❊ ❊ ❊

Nine and a half months after our marriage we had a daughter. One year and one month later we had a son.

The doctor told us no intercourse for the last two months of gestation. I had gotten used to having sex every day and it was difficult for me doing without.

Bonnie felt sorry for me. One day she really surprised me, telling me she could fix me up with one of her girlfriends just temporally to ease my pain. The girl that she was talking about was very attractive. Temptation was after me again. Before Bonnie it was easy to control. I remember once a veterinarian told me that once a male dog has sex he is much more motivated for more. I told her, "no", thanks any way. If Jesus could turn down the devil's offer to have the world I can turn down this. However it did make me wonder about my wife.

I was working nights with one man and three women. The man was married and was going out to the parking lot with one of the women for half an hour each night. I never asked what they were doing; But, I could guess. The other two women gave me a lot of hints about going out after work. One was married. Her husband sold shoes at Sears. She was very good looking, a real temptation for me in my present situation. The other one was widowed. She was about forty years old. She was always very friendly with me. One night she told me, "I would never go out with a married man unless he was sure that it would not adversely affect his marriage."

Yes, I was tempted. My rectum felt like someone had placed a tight fitting rod in it. Is this the way people live? No wonder the divorce rate is so high. If I had given in to temptation, would I likely have done it again and again? Only Jesus could keep me from it.

CHAPTER 3

We had become friends with neighbors behind our house, Chuck and Carol. They invited us over for a drink. They didn't notice that each time I made myself a mixed drink, I mixed all non-alcoholic liquids. I had been in similar situations before and had always had just as much fun as the drinkers.

As the evening went on people got louder and Bonnie was showing a lot of attention to Chuck. I suggested, "I think it is about time for us to go home."

Bonnie replied, "Chuck is going home with me," as she tugged on his belt.

Carol looked at me with a look of approval. She wanted me.

Chuck finally said, "Bonnie, we have had a lot of fun tonight. Now the party is over and it is time for you and your husband to go home."

"But I don't want to go home with my husband. I go home with him every night. What do you think Carol? Would you like to have Kirk stay here with you?"

Carol said, "Please don't get me mixed up in this. It is up to you and Chuck to figure out what is going to happen."
I spoke in a loud voice," I am going home. You are going with me, and Chuck is staying here with his wife"

We left.

* * *

We moved to the San Fernando Valley into a 4,350 square feet house.

I had finished my master's degree and was well on my way to a PhD.

After the children started school, Bonnie went to work.

Bennie's first job was in the accounting department of a large aircraft company 15 miles away. She had only been there a few months when I received a phone call from one of her fellow workers. "Kirk, My name is Rita. I work with your wife. My neck is stuck out a mile calling you."

"Then, I assume, it must be important."

"Yes, it is. And I would not be doing this if you two didn't have two children. I went through a similar thing with my husband five years ago. We had two children also. No one tipped me off, and it went too far. Far enough that our marriage could not be saved."

I think you are about to tell me something ."

"Kirk, there is a test pilot here with whom Bonnie spends her lunch period. I have noticed that she eats a little at a time on the job, so when lunch time comes around, she is already finished with her lunch. So they surreptitiously meet at the exit to the parking lot. Yesterday, I followed at a distance, slipped up behind his pick up and they were kissing and hugging."

"Thank you very much Rita. I will put a quick end to this romance."

I was on spring break from school. I packed up some cloths for me and the children. After leaving a note that simply stated that she had her choice;

'Me and the children or the test pilot'. We went to my mother's house 40 miles away. I explained to mother all of the details and asked her to tell Bonnie when she calls that she could get a message to me. A few hours later she called. Mother took the message. I did not respond for two days. When I got Bonnie on the phone, "Hello, how is your love life."

"I am very sorry Kirk. You should beat me"

"I have no interest in vindictiveness. I just want assurance from you that it is over and will not happen again. You married me in the church. You promised before God that that you forsake all others until death."

"I know. What a fool I have been."

"I want you to quit your job and have someone else tell Frank (the pilot) that if he does not stay away from you I will talk to his wife. Is that clear?"

"Yes."

* * *

I cut back on my school hours and accepted a position as a consultant in a small company in East Los Angeles. It was a long drive to and from the West end of the San Fernando Valley. After a few weeks I arranged to exchange driving with two engineers at the company. When it was not my turn to drive, Bonnie would often drop me off at the home of whom ever was going to drive. One day she had taken our car into the dealer for a 5,000 mile check-up.

When she picked me up that afternoon, I could smell liquor on her breath. Looking at her, she was different. I could tell she had been drinking. I asked "Do you feel OK? What is the problem?"

"I went to the doctor after the car dealer and he gave me a strong shot."

"You had better let me drive."

The next day when I got home from work two of my adult neighbors were roller skating on the side walk. I chatted with them for a few minutes. They told me how beautiful that Cadillac was that was parked in my drive way that day.

I went in the house, received a greeting from the dog, and the children, and a cold hello from Bonnie.

I said," Bonnie, after the children are in bed I want to have a serious talk with you."

She just looked at me. She knew well what the subject would be.

"Do you want to try a second time to tell me what happened yesterday?"

"I was at the car dealer when our salesman saw me and started a nice conversation with me. He went away. Came back an hour or so later. He asked if I would like to go to the club nearby for a drink? I had nothing better to do so I made a mistake and said, "Yes." That was it. He brought me back to the dealership. I got my car and drove away."

"My source tells that a little different (pretending to having her watched). By the way were you aware that yesterday was the fifth anniversary of our wedding."

"Yes, I knew. It made it seem more important"

I said, "You believe sexual immorality, unfaithfulness, and just sin in general is more enjoyable on a special day when it will hurt your husband the most."

No. I don't know what I was thinking."

"How long was he here today?"

"What makes you?......How do you know? Do you have me followed everywhere I go?"

"You have not answered my question. How long was he here today?"

"About half an hour. He asks if I could spend the night with my grandmother sometime."

"In other words, spend the night with him."

"I think that is what he met."

"What did you say?"

"I said I would think about it."

"Bonnie, I don't know why you married me and had my children. You are sick, mentally. I know what you told me years ago, that your father was a very cold man that gave you no personal attention as you were growing up.

Many convicts on trial blame their childhood as justification for their crimes. This is not a consideration for them and it is not for you. Please start with the Pastor of our church and/or our family doctor get into a program of counseling. Do something, and get started right away. If there is one more case of adultery or intended adultery, I will take the children and see to it that you never see them or me again. Is that clear? Also, I picked up my bible, and read Proverbs 5, '*My son pay attention to my wisdom, listen well to my words of insight, that you may maintain discretion and your lips may preserve knowledge. For the lips of an adulteress drip honey, and her speech is smoother than oil; but in the end she is bitter as gall.*"

Bonnie said, "Yes, I will."

* * *

Bonnie got counseling and quickly became a fine wife and mother (for a while).

Since we had moved to The San Fernando Valley we had given up the teen group at our church in the beach area.

Bonnie and I each joined the scouts, I the Cubs and she the Brownies.

I had also taken the job as Chairman of the Board of Christian Stewardship at our church.

I finished school.

We had a swimming pool put in the back yard.

* * *

I had written a term paper for a political science class, the year before on the subject of, *'Right to Work Laws'*. The university sought and obtained my permission to photo copy it and make it available to the student body. A Los Angeles city councilman had obtained a copy and sent someone to my house to invite me to a Republican Party meeting.

To my surprise, when arriving at the meeting, we were asked to sit in the front row. At one point during the meeting someone asked the MC when the speaker would be there. He said, he is here and made a gesture toward me. I did not mind because it was a subject that I knew well. I was told first how much they appreciated my being there. They had asked a few local unions to furnish a speaker. All refused.

"A proposition is on the next ballot. If it passed, it would outlaw the union shop in California. "People who favor the organization of labor were planning to vote against and those who oppose unions were planning to vote in favor. This is very wrong. It is a gross misunderstanding. This proposition if passed will not eliminate or even reduce union membership in California. Let me ask for a show of hands-how many of you live in a neighborhood with CC&R's, that is restrictions that are enforced, usually, by a home owners association? Looks like a little more than half of you. Those CC&R's are for the protection of all property owners. You may say, I am going build an eight feet fence around my front yard. I own the property and it is mine to do with as I please. You will be required to take it down. You will likely be fined in increasing amount each month until it is down. The home owners association may hire an outside contractor to take it down and send you the bill which if you refuse to pay, it becomes a lien on your title with accumulating interest.

If you own the property this is awful. If you are a neighbor you are thankful for the contract. If you think about it, we are loaded with laws that limit some for the benefit of others. What does this have to do with unions? A lot .

We have The Closed Shop, The Union Shop, and The Open Shop. The Closed Shop is commonly practiced by the movie industry, the medical community, and the bar association. Closed simply means that one must join as a condition of employment. That is, join then go to work or start practicing.

The Union Shop is commonly practiced by The Airline Pilots Association, The United Auto Workers, United Mine Workers, and so on. Your Republican candidate for the US Senate has a commercial running on television that shows a group of workers each saying he would join a different union. Well, first of all an employer is only required to negotiate with one union per the Taft/Hartley Labor law, and second can you imagine how confusing it would be to have several unions in one company. From labor's point of view the fear is, 'Divide and conquer'. Your candidate is the laughing stock. The proposed law will fail and your candidate will fail with it unless you can figure some way to separate the two in the minds of the voters."

I would never have guessed that night how much speaking I would be doing before groups in the future. That was my first time speaking to a group other than in class. I would have to be persuasive and keep the groups attention.

They started that night to find ways to free the candidate from the proposition. They were too late. The proposition failed as did their candidate. Shortly after the election the candidate, William F. Knowland, committed suicide.

They stayed in contact. Later I was asked to be treasurer for this local Republican chapter. I had to turn it down because I was too busy with church, scouts and my job.

Later Bonnie and I were invited to dinner with the governor. We accepted and were seated next to him.

Next they invited us to dinner with a little known congressman. We already had plans and turned down the invitation. A few years later we were sorry we had turned it down when this little known congressman was elected President of the United States.

* * *

Bonnie accepted a job at a large manufacturing company just a few miles from home. We attended a party at the home of one of her coworkers. I was not impressed with the group. They were all drinkers and they like to tell dirty jokes. I doubt if there was one Christian in the group.

The following Saturday night we went to my mother's house for dinner. Bonnie said, " I don't feel good, I am going to have to go back home."

I responded, "Wait, we will all go."

"That is not fair to your mother. You and the kids stay."

"Wait Bonnie, let's leave the children and you and I will go. If you don't feel good, I will be there to help you."

"Kirk, you don't seem to understand. I want to be alone."

"What can I say? Good bye."

She returned late the next morning. We all missed Sunday school and church.

Monday morning I received a phone call from one of her fellow workers that I had met at the party at her house. "I wish you would get that God damn wife of yours out of here."

"What is the problem, Barbara?"

"Saturday night we all went out on the town. Had a bit too much to drink. Bonnie said you would not come because you figured you were a bit better than we are. Any way she spent much of the evening rubbing her tits all over my husband. She stayed all night at my house. After my old man and I went to bed, I fell right to sleep. I woke up a couple of hours later. He was not in bed. I went into the living room and found him standing in front of your little sweetie. She was sitting up with her hands on his ass and I hate to tell you what she had in her mouth………Are you still there?"

"Yes, I am here."

"Kirk, Get the kids and get out. Go someplace where she can't find you."

I started thinking again about divorce. I had the hard headed belief that, 'What God has joined together, let no man put under'. I prayed for God's guidance's. Oh, Lord what shall I do? Before leaving, I let a note on the kitchen table, "Bonnie, I can't understand you. We have two fine children.

I have provided you with a beautiful house. My sexual motivation is much higher than yours. Are you trying to find out why you don't enjoy sex?"

"I am unable to come up with the right words, so I will quote from the Bible. *Matthew* 5;27 and 29, *'You have heard that it was said, 'Do not commit adultery. 'If your right eye causes you to sin, gouge it out and throw it away. It is better for you to lose one part of your body than for your whole body to be thrown into hell.'*"

I let my mother know where the children and I would be. We checked into a motel. Fortunately, I was between assignments and could stay with the children.

We had hardly gotten checked in when my mother knocked on the door. "Here is the number. Phone your doctor."

I phoned immediately and learned that Bonnie had attempted suicide.

I let the children stay with their grandmother and drove directly to the hospital. She was sleeping. Dr Findgold said he wanted to keep her overnight.

He wanted to know what I had done to bring her to this point.

She had placed wet towels around the doors, turned on the gas and laid on the kitchen floor. While lying there she phoned one of her boyfriends. Fortunately he sensed her voice was fading, and phoned the fire department. They broke down an outside door, resuscitated Bonnie and beckoned an ambulance.

* * *

Bonnie retained a local attorney for a divorce. I told her that I had studied enough law that I felt confident that I would not need an attorney. The three of us met at his office. We had three houses. She wanted one. She wanted our only car. I was left with a motor cycle. She felt that the children would be better off with me as long as she had visitation rights.

He said he would be ready for signatures in two days.

That night she cried for almost two hours. I stayed away with the children at the other end of the house. After putting the little ones to bed, I sat and started reading my bible. She came in and sat across the room from me and said, "I guess you hate me."

"No, I don't hate you. Your faith is in God's hands."

She promised it would never happen again. We decided to try again.

* * *

Things went well for almost a year. Then one night she went out to 'meet the girls'. She wore a beautiful new dress that I had just bought that day. When she got home it was obvious that she had been drinking.

Two days later she had to leave for work two hours early, she said, because one of her fellow workers was having problems with her husband and she needed to talk. While she was in the bath room I phoned the college student next door. He followed her to where she parked the car, got into a pick up and parked on a lonely road. Judging by their positions they were having intercourse.

Again I let a note, took the children, and went away.

She sealed the house as well as she could, shut off the pilot lights laid on the kitchen floor with a phone in her hand. She phoned her lover who phoned 911. The neighbor next door was a fire man. He broke down the back door. Back to the hospital again.

The next day she returned home. No great agreement; But, We decided to try once more. It lasted several months. We visited her parents a day or two later. Her mother was in tears when she asked Bonnie, "Why do you it. You have two beautiful children, a loyal husband that cares for you like a queen."

"Mother, I just don't know why."

Why did I not divorce her? I always asked myself. Christianity stopped me.

She never blamed me for anything. She always seemed to divert back to the personality that I met in college. I believe she really did try to change. And she could for a while; But it was never more than two years. Was I the one that was wrong? Do people mix it up sexually and just don't talk about it? I remember when I was 13 years old. My mother was working nights. I spent every evening with our next door neighbor. She was 22, had two children, her husband was in the Navy and was gone most of the time.

She made it clear that she wanted to have sex with me. At that age, I was never tempted.

Bonnie rested for a few weeks, and then accepted a job as a teller at a local bank. Having a college degree probably helped her get a couple of rapid promotions. The problem with Bonnie in a job dealing with the public, it provided too much opportunity to meet men. She was still as beautiful or even more beautiful than when we met. Men would stand in long lines just to get close to her.

At Bonnie's suggestion, we all four went to a psychologist that was closely associated with the Los Angeles court system. He met briefly with the four of us, then alone with each of the children, then the children together. Then he spoke to Bonnie and me together. When we got out of his office, she roughly grabbed each of the children, telling them, "Don't you ever come complaining to me about you father again."

* * *

She registered for two night classes at a local college. Every Tuesday and Thursday nights she would bathe and get too pretty for a class.

After several months, that big Sunday walk-out came. A few days after she left, I looked at her school supplies and learned she had registered and attended each class one time. As she departed she left the note.

CHAPTER 4

Lee and Donnelda were raised in the church, Sunday school almost every week. Lee's Sunday school teacher told me that his attention span was quite limited, and that he seem to day dream during class and was unable to answer simple questions about the class current work.

Lee's teacher called me once for a meeting. She suggested that he should have organized type projects at home because in class he seems to always be thinking something other than what he should be thinking about. I wondered then and I still wonder, why he was such a problem in school.

During one semester he attended three different schools. The second one was clearly posted that students were not permitted to leave the school grounds during recess. The first day of school he was caught violating this rule. Talk all I want, did no good. I would ask him, "Lee, since you get up, have breakfast, and go to school why not listen to whatever the teacher is talking about, bring your homework assignments home and do them."

He said,"You don't know what it is like."

His mother and I decided to put him in military school. We thought this was the panacea. The school policy was if a student made less than a "C" in any class a notice would be sent via mail to the parents and the student would have to run up a hill several times arms stretched over head, carrying a rifle. After a few weeks, we were very pleased, that is until I phoned the school and learned that several unsatisfactory notices had been sent home. Lee had been getting the mail.

He got straight F's on every report card until his mother and I divorced.

I thought of Timothy 1;5, *the goal of this command is love, which comes from a pure heart and a good conscience and a sincere faith.* A mother's love is very important to a boy. Lee was receiving none. I believed that he was rebelling.

Donnelda did better than her brother in school. She made "C's" and "B's"

Except for one semester when I worked closely with her. Bonnie suggested that I leave her alone. I went over her homework each night, quizzing her until she could give the right answers. She was thrilled when she would come home with "A's".

Lee was learning in school, yes: But he was learning the wrong things.

One semester he brought home a report card with one "B", one "D" and all the rest "C's" with teacher comments stating "improving, doing better, etc."

Different colors of ink and different hand writing. It was a good forgery. But not good enough. After reading it I shook my head, and looked at him. He cried and through his tears said," I finally got a good report card and you don't believe me."

* * *

Per an arrangement with the school that Lee was then attending, they called to let us know that he had not shown up for school that day. I notified a friend at the police department. That afternoon we received the phone call from the Los Angeles Police Department that Lee had been picked up about ten miles from home. He was being held in jail. After some conversation, we agreed that a night in jail may be good for him. I picked him up the next morning.

A few weeks later, I received a phone call from the Los Angeles Police Department. "Your son shot a boy at the park. We are holding him. We would like for you to come here". My car was in for service, so I got on my motor cycle and headed for the Police Department. I don't remember the trip.

After all I had gone through with this boy this was too much. I collided with a car, and was taken to the hospital I spent three weeks in there. A compression bandage on one hand, and the other arm in a cast. The cast was with me for almost a year.

Two weeks later, Lee and I attended a probation meeting. After the probation officer had asked a few questions, I showed him the note that Bonnie had left. An admission of adultery was enough for him. He ordered that Lee was to live with me, and Bonnie was to have visitation rights pre-approved by me and in my company.

* * *

Court

Three weeks later Lee and I met his mother at Los Angeles County Juvenile Court. The presiding judge looked like she weighted over two hundred pounds. Looking around, I counted three bad boys and one bad girl. The bailiff called the first case, "Los Angeles County vs. Lee W. Donaldson."

The judge asked, "Are both parents present."

I stood and said, "Yes you honor."

The judge stated, "I have a rather complete history of Lee here.

Let me begin with that. You have done poorly on your school work and have been a constant discipline problem in all of your classes. Is this about right Lee? Do you agree with this report?"

"Yes your honor, I agree."

"Your IQ is sufficient for you to make average grades. And with a little added effort you can make above average grades. Do you have things that are more important to do than to study and bring up your grades?"

"No your honor."

"Then, if I ask you to return at the end of next semester with a report card to show to me, what can I expect to see?."

"Nothing less than a C."

"Now the matter for which you were arrested. You took a gun from its rightful owner in Riverside County, brought it to Los Angeles County,

Took it to the park, and while playing with other boys shot one of the boys. Is this about what happened Lee?

"Yes your honor."

"This is on top of a long list of felonious behavior. I could send you to juvenile detention for six months. You are lucky that the boy suffered only a minor wound. And you and your parents are lucky that his parents are not suing."

Lee, I am going to sentence you to six months in juvenile detention. However with your promise that you will pay attention in each of your classes in school, do your homework, obey your custodial parent, don't steal anything, I will suspend your sentence. Can you do this Lee? Do I have your promise?"

"Yes your honor"

"Bonnie Donaldson, I have a rather complete history on you here also. Since you are not on trial, I am not going to read any of it. Instead I understand that the probation department recommended that Mister Donaldson have custody of Lee, and that you have visitation rights only with Mister Donaldson's approval, and in his presents. Is that your understanding?"

"Yes."

"The probation department can only make recommendations. This court hereby orders the probation department's recommendation. This will be in force until you can show the court that you have made a major change in your life style."

"Mister Donaldson, the reports show that you are a very good disciplinarian. Please keep up the good work."

"Thank you your honor"

"Next case"

CHAPTER 5

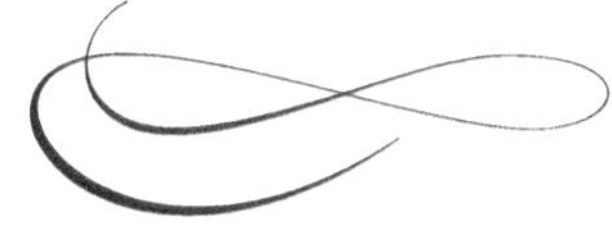

An immediate change took place in Lee's attitude and behavior. I will never know whether this was due to the absence of Bonnie, or the Judge's order. I thanked God for this change. Donnelda was living a school semester with her maternal grandparents. Lee appreciated the calm that existed in the house. I don't think he understood what caused the tranquility. Once he suggested," Just leave my sister at Grandma house." Each morning the first one in the kitchen prepared breakfast for both. I made regular trips to school, visiting with his teachers. It was the first time that he made "C's" and "B's".

When the school semester was over, I drove the 60 miles to pick up Donnelda. Bonnie was there with my replacement. Bonnie had little to say. But Bonnie's mother and step father had a lot to say. They tried their best to get me to leave Donnelda there for a week, a month or a few months. I have to admit, I enjoyed my position. For the first time I was totally in charge. After each had their say, I simply said, "She is going home now."

One night, Donnelda stayed at a girl friend's house. I went out, leaving Lee at home with one of his friends. The two boys went to a house that was under construction caused a lot of damage. This did not become known to me for a few days. The next day he went to the beach with a neighbor and her son. When they returned near home, Lee saw a police car parked in front of our house. He assumed that it was related to the house break in. Actually it was a personal friend that I had met in a club that I had recently joined. Lee did not come home. I had no idea where he was. I put in a missing person's report the next day. That evening, I got a knock on my door. It was the general contractor of the damaged house. He informed me of the damage and told me that someone had seen my son leaving the house. I offered to pay him for the damage. But he refused.   He only wanted me to know so I could take disciplinary action.

Lee had been gone about a month, when I got a call from the police. They had found him. He had been living three blocks away at the home of a friend of his. I talked to the police about what I should do. After many considerations, I decided to ask the police to not bring criminal charges against the parents because it would end up in court, the juvenile court judge would learn about it, and Lee would have to serve six months. However, as time went by, I realized that I had made a mistake.

CHAPTER 6

When Bonnie left, she believed that she had finally found the love of her life. I hoped she had. After sixteen years of emotional strain, I shall always remember this as the happiest day of my life. Worry was gone. I was free. A few days later, I filed for divorce. It was uncontested. She did not show in court, and made no attempt to get the children. I received title to our three houses, both cars, and custody of the children. Later, I deeded one of the houses to her and gave her one of the cars.

The day after she moved out, I told my fellow workers. Two of them quickly recommended a so-cial club for people who have been married and have children. I looked in the white pages for **PARENTS WITHOUT SPOUSES** (PWS). I was told that Friday night of that week was an orientation meeting for potential members.

The meeting was at a home on Rodeo Drive in Beverly Hills. I thought I had a big house. Mine could all fit in the living room of that place. The very friendly hostess was Jewish. I had almost no experience with Jews socially or professionally. The president, also Jewish, introduced himself, gave a brief explanation of the purpose of the club and passed out programs of the months activities. "The club is international. Our local chapter has over 1,000 members. Our primary purpose is to provide activities for our children. We have picnics, beach outings, parties, and many other activities for you to bring your children. Our club is for parents who are divorced, legally separated, or widowed. It is not necessary that you have custody of your children. We have a sub group, Tiny Tots, specifically for children that see the non-custodial parent less than once a year. Also, we have a teen age group. If you look at your bulletins, you will see that we have group discussions, one almost every night. Once per month, we have a dance and also a general meeting. We try to have a party each month. Now I have a request. We need someone to volunteer a house for a party next month. The house should accommodate 150 people. We have a cleaning crew that will clean your house after the party. Also there is an opening for a leader of our teen age group. If you would like to learn more about either one of these, please see me when we break for refreshments. Thank you for coming. I will be here with the other officers to answer any questions."

I quickly went forward and introduced myself. "Sounds like you have enough activity to keep everyone busy. I have a house that will hold 150 and I would like to offer it for next month's party. Also after we know each other better, I would like to be considered for chairman of teen age activities. My wife and I headed a teen age group in our church."

During the social hour that followed I noticed that the women out numbered the men two to one. Several of the women gave me very friendly looks. I could not believe that any woman would have an interest in me. For 16 years my wife had told me that I was a country hick. As a potential lover, I had a very low opinion of myself. I honestly believed that if the ugliest, fattest, oldest woman there would have dated me, I would have felt lucky.

An attractive woman seemed to be headed straight for me. She looked to be in her late twenties, was about 5'4", and had a beautiful complication. Her skin seemed to be naturally tan, nose was just a little too big; But, That made her look cute. She wore a bright dress that fell just above her knees, a matching jacket and black stiletto heels.

She said, "Would you like a glass of punch? My name is Clair Norman and I see you are Kirk (looking at my paper name tag). How did you learn about us?"

*I had been married for 16 years. Then I had been without a wife for five days. I was what was called, '**a babe in the woods**'. This is the first good looking girl that has approached me since college single days.*

"Yes, very nice of you Clair" As we walked to the punch table I said,   "A fellow worker told me that I was eligible for membership in **PWS**. What is your responsibility in the club?"

"I am vice president.

"The punch is good; But, I think it has been spiked with a little vodka." I had never tasted vodka before. But I had smelled it. "And what does the vice president do?"

"Not much. You see, I am a full time student at UCLA. I have a few months to go to get my PhD in clinical psychology. I stand in for the pres when he is not available, I moderate some group discussions. Look at your bulletin. You will see my name in there a few times."

"The group seems to be very Jewish."

"It is about half. I am Jewish. What kind of work do you do?"

"I am a physicist. I work contract, mostly Federal Government."

"It was nice of you to volunteer your house for next month's party."

"My house can fit 150; but it will be a little tight."

"I think you will enjoy the club. Your personality and education will fit well. I must circulate and meet the other guests. Don't let any of the ladies take advantage of you. My phone number is in the bulletin if you ever want to get , ah, I mean if you have any questions."

As Clair walked away, I spotted a very nice looking young lady sitting alone at the other end of the room. As I was walking toward her, I thought about what one of the guys at work had told me about the club, "One can meet girls in a library, a gym, school, but at none of these places can you feel that they want to meet men. At **PWS** you can bet they are there to meet men." I looked around the room and thought these women are here to meet me.

This one appeared to be about 25 years old, olive complexion, very well dressed. I sat next to her, and said, "My name is Kirk. I thought you looked lonely sitting here. I hope you don't mind."

"Not at all. My name is Yesinia. I am new around here."

"Where is here? You mean the Los Angeles area?"

"Yes that too. But what I mean is I am new to the United States."

"And you are from where?"

"I am from Mexico, Mexico City."

This lady was beautiful. "There is a party tomorrow night. Are you planning to go?"

"I would like to go; But, I fear going alone. My parents were very strict. I was brought up with the understanding that I never go out unescorted."

"I have not had a date for about 17 years. I don't know the proper way to ask. Well, here goes, May I escort you to the party?"

"You seem like a gentleman. I would be happy to go to the party with you."

Later, I learned one never takes a date to a PWS party.

* * *

The president was obviously looking at me from across the room. After getting Yesinia's address, and properly excusing myself, I headed across the room. "Mister President."

"Please don't call me Mister President. My name is Harold Morris. Clair told me that she was impressed with you. I want you to know that I am pleased that you are considering leadership of the teen age group and also that you are going to let us use your house for next month's party.

"I guess that is the way to get to know people."

"Well, I am going to give you an opportunity to get to know all of the officers. We are having a private party for officers only, one week from tomorrow night. I would like to have you come. "Well, I am going to give you an opportunity to get to know all of the officers. We are having a private party for officers only, one week from tomorrow night. I would like to have you come.

Your application states that you are 36 years old, recently divorced, have a 14 year old daughter and a 13 year old son. As I said earlier, the primary purpose of the club is to provide for our children. Divorce and death of a parent are hard on our children. We try to give them every opportunity to be with children that have gone through the same experience."

"As I told you, my wife and I led a teen group in my church; But, They were all from families with two parents. So this will be for whomever is chosen, a challenges".

CHAPTER 7

When Yesinia and I arrived at the party, We were greeted at the door by half a dozen or so people. 'What a friendly bunch', I thought. Two ladies that were at the orientation the night before walked across the room to greet us. One said, "We felt sorry for Yesinia last night and tonight she walks in with this hunk." I was not familiar with the word, hunk.

The house was about the same size as my house. But it did not look like a family home. More like a business. After the foyer was a large room with tables, folding tables, with folding chairs. A few months later I learned that this was a typical house for many divorced people, i.e., One person got the house and the other got the furniture. I took a table. As I was sitting down, I noticed an unpleasant look on Yesinia's face. Two, what appeared to be, Mexican ladies were sitting next to me. We talked for a little while. I danced with Yesinia twice. I never asked any one else to dance.

Back at the table, I asked, " Would you like a drink?"

"Yes", she said, and named the drink. Some kind of cocktail that I had never heard of and soon forgot. I went to the bar, got a seven up for myself. I explained to Yesinia that the bar tenders had never heard of the drink that she had requested; But, They do have bourbon, scotch, and vodka that can be mixed with water, seven up, or coke. She decided to have a coke which I promptly got for her. I had my first bourbon and coke. I thought, It taste good and gave me a light headed feeling.

I noticed a few people had plates of food. One of the Mexican ladies said it was time to eat. Yesinia told me what she wanted to eat just like I was her waiter. One of the ladies at our table smiled and said, " The way it is done at club functions is the men get the drinks and the women get the food. "

Yesinia asked me, "Are you going to get my food?"

I replied, "Are you going to get my food?"

"No", she quickly said.

The woman sitting next to me said, "Kirk, I will get a plate for you."

Yesinia, looking angry said, "I am ready to leave."

After I ate my food, we left.

"Humbled Mexican trash", she said as soon as we got into the car.

"I don't understand. You are Mexican yourself and you talk about these Mexican ladies like that."

"There should be separate clubs. In Mexico, I never associated people like that." "Do you think you are better than they?" "Depends on what is better. I am educated, come from a fine family, we lived in a beautiful house, and had nice cars to drive. The only association that I had with the lower class was they worked in our house and yard cleaning, cooking, yard work, washing the cars, and so on."

I was driving toward her home when after a long silence she spoke, "I would like a cup of coffee."

I don't believe she knew how irritated I was with her. But I was well trained in taking a lot of crap from a woman.

"OK, I'll take you to a coffee shop."

She waited until I went around to open the door for her. She was not at all friendly in the coffee shop. When we arrived at her house, I, of course, opened the car door for her and walked her to her front door. She stood and looked eye to eye at me, she was anticipating something. I wondered what she wanted me to do. I put my hands on her shoulders. She didn't move. Just kept staring. I leaned forward and gave her a very light, very short kiss, told her good night and walked away.

About a year later, I saw Yesinia at a party in Hollywood. She gave me a dirty look and did not speak. This was what I expected because a friend that owned a Mexican restaurant had once remarked that I had done something bad to Yesinia. She was a disappointing first date.

As *the months and years went by I learned a lot about women. Times had changed a lot in the 16 years that I had been married. I learned that the biggest change was the birth control pill. Women had become more aggressive. How am I going to deal with this? I am a Christian. I am also highly motivated sexually. Can I get involved sexually and still love the Lord? I think of the 138th psalm, 'Even if I walk into trouble, you will keep my life safe. You will put out your hand against the anger of those who do not like me.'*

CHAPTER 8

I phoned one of the secretaries at a company where I had worked. She was unmarried, about 15 pounds overweight, approximately my age, maybe a little older. I learned at work that she was easy to talk to. After Yesinia, I needed a nice normal lady just to talk to.

She arrived at the house half an hour later. She looked really nice. She said, "Kirk, what a beautiful house you have. You have two children?"

"They are spending the week end with my mother. It was very nice of you to come tonight. I am very happy to finally be free of my wife; But, I needed someone to talk with."

"You have only been separated seven days. You say you are happy, but it is still an adjustment. Have you done anything to develop a social life?"

"Yes, I have. I joined **PWS.** Went to an organization meeting. Met a beautiful young lady. Took her to a party last night. She was not very nice."

"Why do you say, she was not very nice?"

I told her every detail about that night.

"Well Kirk, I hate to tell you. I know what the problem was. You have only been split a week. I'll bet she has been split a bit longer. The reason most people go to a singles club is companionship. Her asking for a cup of coffee was her way of telling you that she was not in a hurry to get home. If you had asked her if she would like to see your house, she would have said yes."

"You are telling me that she was, ah, ah, interested, ah, she had hot pants?"

"You were married 16, 17 years. Women have changed a lot in those years. They have the same drives as men. Since the pill came out they have been emancipated. Especially in a club like **PWS.**

When a couple breaks up the one that leaves usually has someone else. So they have no reason to go to a club to meet someone. The ones that you will meet at **PWS** are just like you. They have been jilted. Some want to prove that they are sexually capable. Some want to get even with the x-spouse by having several sex partners. Kirk, sex is the name of the game. Get used to it."

"I believe you, but it is very hard for me to accept. I am highly motivated sexually. I have always been able to keep it under control. Before I was married, I had many opportunities. I believed and still believe that sex is for marriage."

"What church do you attend?" She asked.

"I don't believe that denomination is important. Right now, I am going to a Lutheran church. But my rigid beliefs toward sex are from the Bible."

"I am Catholic and I am not married and I am not as rigid as you. You are going to have some difficulty Kirk. Show me the rest of your house."

"Oh, of course, pardon me for not offering before." We walked through every room. The last room that we were in was the master bed room.

"A king sized bed. Do you sleep in this big bed by yourself?"

"No, sometimes my German Sheppard sleeps with me."

She stood there and stared at me. Her eyes had a sparkle in them. She put her arms around me and held me tightly. Immediately I thought of the many ladies at church who would hug me as a greeting. However they were not in my bedroom next to my bed. Then I thought how nice of Marge to hug me when she knew I was not emotionally at my best. But then on the other hand I could feel her large breasts against my chest and the warmth of her body. I had not had any sex for weeks and I could feel my erection pressing against her. She sat on the bed with me standing in front of her. She unzipped my pants loosened my belt and let my pants fall. She had a little difficulty getting my shorts down over my erection. She kissed it, rubbed it against both of her cheeks, licked it, and put it in her mouth for just about a minute. Then she said, "Just a little. Would you like to have sex with me?"

I couldn't say no.

She unbuttoned and removed my shirt. I kicked off my shoes.

She asked, "Are you going to make me take off my own clothes?"

"May I help you?"

She just nodded her head.

I pulled up her sweater and looked at those beautiful big tits. I unsnapped her bra and pulled it off her shoulders. I couldn't wait. I fondled them and got down on my knees, and kissed and licked them. I removed the rest of her cloths, folded back the blankets and we laid down. She felt so good in my arms. I laid on her as she guided it in. She climaxed a few seconds before I did.

I thought, "Oh God, could this be wrong? So natural and it felt so good."

"Well Kirk, what did you think about that."

"That was the best that I have had in about 16 years."

We just laid there arm in arm with me occasionally kissing a breast.

* * *

Friday evening I received a phone call from Clair. "How are you this evening Kirk? Harold told me that he invited you to the officer's party. Are you planning to go?"

"Yes, I plan to go. You, of course will be there. Right?"

"It is going to be close to my home. Would you mind picking me up?"

Saturday night, at my car, I started to walk on the passenger side obviously to open the door for her. She stopped me and said, "No Kirk, I am a big girl and I can open the door for myself."

I hurried around the other side, got in, sat down, and looked over just as she was getting in. Her skirt went half way up her thigh when she sat down. For just a few seconds I stared at her beautiful legs. Then I don't know what came over me as I leaned over and kissed one of them. No reaction from her.

About fifteen women and ten men were in attendance at a very nice house in Granada Hills. Our hostess, Joyce Axle, introduced herself. Clair introduced me to many others. I had a mixed, alcoholic drink.

Harold announced that it was time to play a game. He named two women that could stay in the room that we were in with all of the men. The other women were sent to another room. Then four pillows were laid end to end on the floor. One Woman, blind folded was brought out of the other room. She was escorted by two men, one on each side, as she straddled the pillows. As soon as she got to the end of the row of pillows two men lay on their backs on the pillows. Her blind fold was removed. The two women that were aloud to stay were wearing slacks. The reaction of the women was different. I guess it was, at least, partly determined by weather they were wearing under pants.

I used the master bath. Lifting the toilet seat I noticed a note attached to the bottom side. It said, "Hooray, there is a man in the house."

I met April at the party. She was very interesting. Lived nearby. Had two children. Was obviously well educated. Nice figure. I let her know that I was impressed with her. She replied by saying that she had a dark side. Later I learned about the dark side and was shocked.

"Can I get a drink for you?", I asked as she got to the end of the row of pillows

"Yes, a plain 7-up."

I got her 7-up, and a bourbon and seven for myself.

The party started slowing down. People were leaving. I saw Clair across the room looking my way. I went over grabbed her hand. Said good bye to several people.

When we got in my car, I put my arms around her and we kissed. It was not the kind of kiss one gave to ones parents. It was the hottest kiss to date for me. I let go and drove away.

She said, "Kirk, we can take off our cloths, get in bed, and hold each other close. But, that is all I can do."

" I understand."

When we got into her bedroom, she put her arms around me and planted another hot kiss on me. She took her fancy bed spread off her king sized bed, carefully folded it , and placed it on a bench at the foot of the bed. The covers were carefully pulled to the foot of the bed. I thought, she is making a big play area for us to just hold each other. She left me there, and went into another room. As soon as she left I removed all of my cloths and got on her bed.

She came back wearing a rob that she dropped as she got on the bed beside me. I had a strange feeling go through me and I automatically turned away from her. I thought, "Oh Lord what am I doing."

She cuddled against my back. Her body felt so good against my back. Soon one hand was around me and holding my man-hood. I rolled over on to my back. She edged her way half way across me. I raised her up just a little and sucked on both of her breasts. She kissed my chest, then my stomach, and then started licking my penis. Not for long. Soon she had it in her mouth, raising her head up and down. I grabbed her shoulders and rotated us both onto our sides. She never missed a stroke. Now I had her where I could pump my body while I held her head still. About ten minutes of this and I ejected in her mouth.

As I was driving home at about three, the next morning, I was thinking about Clair. What a good time I had with her, and wondering, this woman has a master's degree and almost a PhD. Maybe in my marriage, I was the one who was wrong-not Bonnie. Sex seems so easy to get, and so enjoyable. I thought about the people at the party that night. They are, I am sure, very giving. They work for their children. All of the money that is taken in is used for children's activities. Last night had been their time to have fun, no work, just fun. I wondered, how many of them did what Clair and I did after the party?

⚜ ⚜ ⚜

I phoned April Saturday afternoon. She was quick to invite me to dinner.

Her house was big and beautiful. However, I soon learned it was not her house. April lived with her mother, step father and her two children. And, don't let me forget her German Sheppard.

Before dinner we had cocktails. I had a second.
That wonderful light headed feeling was back.

The dinner was great. Great food that is. I immediately felt sorry for them because none of them said grace before eating. I bowed my head and quickly thanked God. There seems to be a misunderstanding in the minds of many (maybe most) people that one only has to say I am a Christian and believe he or she is going to go to heaven. That is like believing that I am going to be a great professional football player some day even though I currently never touch a football.

After dinner we all sat in the living room and discussed the stock market, and April's daughter's ice skating. She was going to try out for the US Olympic team. They asked about my work. I explained, "Being a contractor, I got used to working part time. I make more money in a few months than an average engineer makes in a year, and I have better tax deductions."

I invited April to go to church with me. I was a little surprised when she said "yes".

Sunday morning April and I walked into church with many people looking our way. Few people realized the many problems that Bonnie and I had. And few knew that we had separated one week before. A few came up to us, gave nice greetings and gestured they wanted to be introduced to my guest. It would have been easy to lie and introduce April as a cousin or niece. But I played it honestly and just introduced her as a friend. Many of these people had been in the *Bethel Series*, a class that I had taught. One lady who was a nurse at a local hospital knew somewhat of the problems that I had had with Bonnie. Once when I was on a job in Duluth, Minnesota, I had a serious eye problem, phoned my doctor who told me to be on the next plane home. My left eye was removed that night. This nurse was there the next morning. She awakened me by hugging me with a warm loving hug. She asked where my wife was, and I told her that Bonnie had a party the night before, that she didn't want to miss, and I suppose that morning she was probably at work. The nurse and her husband sincerely look pleased that I was with a female friend.

The pastor had an appropriate sermon that morning;

"When I was a child, I was rewarded or punished immediately after an act deserving of either. This made the relationship between cause and effect very clear to me. As an adult timing is different. Sometimes I must wait days for the consequences of my behavior. It seemed like God did not care when I misbehaved when days went by without punishment. Something similar happened to the children of Israel; when they disobeyed God and did not receive immediate punishment they believed God had forsaken them.

In Ezekiel, chapter 12, verse 28 God spoke to them, "None of my words will be delayed any longer; whatever I say will be fulfilled." When God seems slow to discipline you, it is not lack of interest, it is the nature of God. God is slow to anger; But don't mistake that, as permission to sin. Instead interpret that as, an opportunity to repent."

I thought a great deal about this sermon and how it related to my life. Can I expect God to punish me for what I had done that week? My sexual motivation was high, and somehow I could not pray for it to be otherwise. Sex was very enjoyable for me. Maybe one might feel guilty with sexual involvement if the chance for pregnancy was given. In my case, that was not a fear because years before I had a vasectomy.

I introduced April to the pastor. He was very happy to meet her. So much so that he invited us to have lunch with him and his wife.

Pastor's wife was a good cook. She and April seem to get along well. After eating, the ladies excused themselves and went into the kitchen. I was glad because that gave me a chance to converse with the pastor. I told him briefly about the many cases of adultery, previous separations and why the latest was the final one. As the old saying goes, I was letting no grass grow under my feet. He indicated that he approved.

I pulled in front of April's house, parked, and killed the engine. She was in no hurry to exit. Seem to have something on her mind. I reached over and grasped her hand. She squeezed it. I held her in my arms. She felt good, at first. Then I sensed her body stiffening. She gently pulled away.

I said, "What is the matter April."

"I know I just met you; but; I have very warm feelings for you. However before things go too far there is something I must tell you. I am ill. I am mentally ill. About half of my life is spent in the mental hospital at Camarillo. I have schizophrenia. I take medication every day."

I asked, "Is the medication effective?"

"Yes, most of the time."

"I remember from one of my psychology classes that according to Sigmund Freud, *All normal people possess all of the characteristics of psychosis and neurosis in varying degrees.*"

"No doubt that is true. But when one is extreme as in my case, it is a problem."

During the next several months, I saw a lot of April. Sigmund had another popular saying, viz., *at the basis of all psychosis and neurosis there will always be found a sexual component.* April certainly verified that. She wanted so much to have sex with me or someone. She could not do it. Once she told me that she was coming to a party at my house, and she was going to have so much to drink that I could do anything I wanted to her.

She spent the last half hour of the party sitting on my lap. After everyone else had gone, I tried to feel a breast. She slapped me. Then I saw tears running down her cheeks as she told me she was sorry.

Every one else had gone. We were alone. Then came a knock at the door. I suspected who it was. So I asked April, "Don't ask any questions. I am going to hide. You answer the door. If it is who I think it is, just tell her that I went out to somewhere. She is about 45 to 50 years old, not very attractive, stringy long grey hair. Make it seem like you live here with me."

April opened the door. It was who I thought it was. April did everything one could imagine to discourage her. But nothing seemed to help. She looked all over the house before finally leaving.

I came out of hiding and explained to April, "This woman, I had worked with several months ago. She was a secretary in an engineering department. She took a shine to me when she heard that I had separated from my wife. I swear she used to wait in the hall way outside of my office just to talk to me. She would put a great deal of effort into trying to convince me that one did not have to be married to have sex. I just acted dumb until it became too much of a problem. So I spoke to her supervisor and finally that corrected the problem."

"A fellow worker of hers, who also was a friend of mine, told her that I was having a party. She phoned to ask me if she could come. Without thinking, I said yes. So when the doorbell rang, I guessed it was she."

April said, "You poor fellow. Women always after you."

"I don't think that is funny. Right now, there is only one woman that I wish was after me."

"I am sorry Kirk."

* * *

I attended my first **PWS** general meeting. Looked like about 400 people in attendance. As expected the women out numbered the men by two to one.

After the business, the chairs were moved and dancing began. I was just standing when a very Jewish young lady walked up and said,

"I thought this was supposed to be for single people. Look. I think almost everyone here has a date."

There was no truth to what she said. I just had to figure out what she meant.

"Yes. They do seem to team up quickly when the dancing started."

Actually, there were over 100 females standing around the edge of the dance floor waiting for someone to ask them to dance. This young lady had the necessary drive to approach a man.

"Can I buy you a drink?"

"Yes. I'll have a 7UP."

She gave me her name, phone number, address, and her family status. She was divorced, had two children, Jewish, live in an apartment in North Hollywood, and her x-husband was a son-of-a-bitch. This description fit the most of the women that I met.

This gal was a little too thin. She looked like Barbara Streisand. She was about five feet, three inches tall, and had a beautiful complication; I guess 29 or 30 years old.

"I am getting a little tired of standing," she said.

"Where would you like to go?"

"I don't care. Just somewhere, where we can sit."

"My car is out in front. Let's start there, and we can decide if we want to go anywhere else."

My Cadillac had an arm rest on the front seat. It was easy to fold up out of the way which is what I did as soon as we got in. We talked for a few minutes. Then I looked at her. She looked at me. Our eyes seem to express the same thing. I reached over slowly, putting one arm behind her and one across her waist. I didn't need to pull her toward me. She was moving quickly toward me. By then I knew, I had a hot one. She sure knew how to kiss. I started feeling her breasts.

"That bra feels beautiful. I would like to taste what it is holding."

"Not tonight. You can see it and taste what it is holding another night."

"When ?"

"Tomorrow."

I made a date for her to come to my house.

Joann was an unusual woman in many ways. Her attitude was no fooling around. Let's get to it. She was always ready. She would close her vagina so tightly that I could not get my finger in. No oral sex.

I later made a count. What percentage of women is affirmative to oral sex? It depends on a few factors. The man for example. I knew one woman that had sex with me and three of my friends. Sam Howard told me that he tried for oral and she said 'no'. Bryan Stevens had the same experience as I and Frank Buck. Sam Howard owned a machine shop and usually had grease under his fingernails. His complication was rough and always looked unclean. Bryan Stevens told me just a little over 50% did give him oral sex. I had a few women tell me that Bryan had an unusually large male organ. After questioning all of my buddies, I came up with 80 to 90 percent of the women had oral sex. About 60 to 65 percent of the women were Jewish. However, I don't believe that was a factor.

. Joann took an interest in my daughter. They developed a great friendship. Once she took my daughter to the mall and bought her several outfits for school. I took her and her two children to a **PWS** camp out. I picked them up and we all spent the night at my house.

The little ones went to bed early, leaving her and me alone in the den. I started moving close on the sofa. She quickly said, "No." This was the first "no" I had gotten from her. She saw the confused look on my face and said,

"Not with the children in the house."

I thought, I would give her credit for good judgment, passing up sex for which she was so highly motivated, for the sake of her children.

I had a couple shots of whiskey before going to bed. It seemed to relieve my feeling of rejection. I liked drinking alcohol. At that time, I never had a thought that it would make a prisoner of me.

The next morning we loaded the tent, camping stove, and other gear into the trunk of the car. It was a beautiful campground

With a little help from the little ones I set up the tent. Her son asked if we were all going to sleep in there. I told him no. It is just for you, your sister and your mother. I will sleep in the car.

That night after the children had gone to bed, Joann and I went for a walk, holding hands, with my arm around her. When we got around the parking lot to my car, I suggested we sit a talk for a while. Knowing how hot she was, she hesitated for just a moment then got in. That was my first experience with sex in the car. She climaxed three times. But, no oral sex.

I went to a little league game in which her son was playing. Her x- husband was there. He sure gave me a dirty look. I wondered why. Soon I was to learn why. Joann told me she would have to pay for having me there.

One night Joann and I went to a private party. She had a bit too much to drink. In her drunken voice she said, "My husband got pissed at me for no good reason. If I could give those men satisfaction, why shouldn't I."

Our relationship just naturally slowed. She showed at my house for the next big **PWS** party. She latch on to a new guy and left the party early with him. I wondered if he will get to see the bra tonight.

Could one cause of divorce be, the husband works very hard during the day? Comes home to a rested wife who had been thinking about sex most of the day?

* * *

Dixie was a sweet, loveable little mother. I met her at a party at my house. She suggested that I come to her house for a short visit the next day. She had two fine children. Dixie invited me to stay for lunch and gave me a bag of fresh homemade chocolate chip cookies to take home. She had a high school education and a year of college. Her figure was outstanding, about 5 feet, six, 115 pounds, nice flat stomach, 34B was my guess for bra size. I asked if she would like to go to a drive in theater with me. She quickly said yes.

The next night I took a pint of scotch to the drive in. The movie depicted a young girl that went in an attic with two young men. They each had sexual relationship with her a few times. I wondered if my date would be offended. Instead she said, "If you're going to go, that is the way to go." as she cuddled up closer to me.

She put a hand on my leg in such a way that I thought she was going to fracture my penis. I said "Careful young lady, you almost broke my penis off."

"Oh, that would have been awful." She said as she felt around for it.

"Do you want me to get it out.", I said.

She did not answer. She just looked at me for a minute or two. Then planted a big kiss on my lips.

As soon as she pulled away I unzipped my pants and took it out of my shorts. This is what she wanted. She scooted her bottom away, then leaned back, took it in one hand and then in her mouth. I had a few swallows from my bottle while she sucked.

This made me wonder. I got married rather young, had only dated a few girls. Have women always been this way. No, I thought. The birth control pill had been out for a few years. That fact seemed to emancipate women. Bonnie had told me a few times about women she worked with; the jokes they told. They were all on the pill. When I think about it now, I realize that most women are very interested in sex. So far, I have proven that to be true. I am lucky to drive a Cadillac with a bench seat rather than one of those cars with bucket seats.

* * *

I met Dixie 3 years later. She was in the foyer of a home that was having a **PWS** party. Dixie was arguing with the man at the door. She was saying that she had belonged to **PWS** a few years before. The man explained that anyone who had already been a member was not permitted to be a guest at any **PWS** function. She would have to join to participate.

I walked over and said, "Hallow Dixie."

"Hi Kirk"

"Sounds like you have a problem."

"Yes, I never realized what this guy is talking about,"

"Let me be of service. I am not involved with anything here. I will be happy to escort you for the rest of this evening." We left in my car and went to a restaurant nearby. She explained that she had gotten married again and was currently going through a divorce. Like most newly divorced persons, she explained, it was all her husband's fault. He insisted that the house must always be neat and clean, everything in its place. She had also returned to school and got a Bachelor of Science in psychology. I invited her to have dinner with me the next night at my house.

The next night she phoned to say that she was having car trouble and in order to come for dinner I would have to transport her. I picked her up. Before dinner, we each had a couple of mixed drinks. We had ground sirloin, mashed potatoes, string beans and pineapple upside down cake. After dinner I started clearing the dishes.

She said, "Don't do that. Just leave them."

"I always clear the table and clean the kitchen after eating."

We went in the living room, sat and talked. She rearranged the throw pillows on the couch. I was sitting across the room from her. I knew that she came for something other than dinner.

I had developed the belief that newly separated people like to have a lot of sex because each had to prove the spouse was wrong in saying they were cold, or simply because they had gone without for a long while during the arguments that brought on the divorce.

I got up from my chair walked across the room, reached down with both hands grasping both of her hands, pulled just a little. She got up hugged me and kissed me. She still had that firm slender body that I remembered three and a half years ago. Just as we started to walk away, I reached down and rearranged the pillows. She immediately said, "Don't."

In the bed room, I slowly removed her clothing, folding and laying each piece neatly. She laid flat on the bed. I put one knee beside her chest and the other over her and on her other side. Her breasts were directly under my butt. As I leaned forward, it was obvious that I expected to put it in her mouth as I had years before. But; She said, "Turn around; I want some of that good licking feeling too". I responded. We climaxed at the same time.

I said, "Well, we can honestly say that we did not have sexual intercourse this night because my penis never touched your vaginal wall".

As soon as we got into my car, she lit a cigarette.

"Sorry Dixie, no smoking in the car ".

She responded by opening the window about 2 inches.
"Dixie, that will not do. I do not allow anyone to smoke in my car".

She moved the window down a little more. I stopped the engine, got out, and walked around the car. I opened the door grabbed her gently by the wrist and started pulling her out. She finally got the idea and dropped the cigarette on the garage floor.

"Thank you Dixie".

Dixie had changed from a very giving person to a very taking person. I didn't believe education had caused that change because of the many very giving, educated ladies that I met.

Needless to say, that was the last time I saw her.

CHAPTER 9

I went to the monthly business meeting of **PWS**. I estimate about 400 attendees. From about the sixth row, I couldn't help but notice two rows in front of me was a beautiful, black haired young lady that appeared to be about 25 years old. Since I was still adjusting to unmarried life, I assumed she would have no interest in me. *(Guess how long it took for me to get over that assumption).*

The meeting went well. The club seem to be well organized with good leadership. I was one of about 30 asked to stand as a new member. I seemed to fit in so well with this group.

God must have felt that when I blended in and lived like those who don't seem to have outspoken love for Him, I could almost hear Him saying, "What are you doing Kirk, living like that? You belong to me."

Clair noticed me from up on the stage. She poked the lady sitting next to her who also looked directly at me.

I wondered, do women tell other women about their sexual encounters? I remembered my ex-wife telling me about some of the stories she heard from her female fellow workers. I never kept a record; But, it seemed like about half of them were having extramarital affairs. This was in the accounting department. Working with engineers and scientists, I can think of only one case of adultery. That was a man with no church home, no interest in Christianity. He had developed a strong interest in one of the other engineers who I learned was homo sexual. Once when my wife was visiting with her parents hundreds of miles away, I mentioned to him that not having sex was bothering me. Much to my surprise he said, "Go over to my house tonight, I will be out all evening."

I didn't go. However a few weeks later I did stop at his house. We were all standing in the kitchen, when he asked if I would like a beer. I said "yes". He left the room. His wife told me to go in the living room and sit on the sofa. A few minutes later she rounded the corner with two beers. She set them both on the coffee table at my knees, sat down tightly against me and asked, " Do I make it hard for you?"

Her husband was sitting at the other end of the room with his back to us watching television.

I don't remember what I answered. As much as I liked alcohol, I don't remember even if I drank the beer. Somehow, I excused myself and left.

These two had set themselves up for what they believe was a short and thrilling life. It was short; But, it was very long if they included the time they will spend in hell. The Bible says that any sexual activity outside of marriage is immoral. This couple should read Genesis 2:24, Exodus 20:14,

1 Corinthians 7:2, Hebrews 13:4. Of course these apply to married people.

* * *

At the conclusion of the meeting, the bar opened and people started socializing. I was on my second drink when a nice looking woman, about 30 to 35 years old, walked up to me and started a conversation. Within just a few minutes, I asked her to meet me at my car, that I described as a new Coupe De Ville, silver-green, and gave the exact location. She agreed without question. The reason I asked her to go ahead of me was because I wanted an opportunity to at least meet the black haired beauty that had been sitting two rows in front of me. I spent a few minutes looking around. Didn't see her, and left.

Valerie was standing by the car waiting. I took her to a Denny's café. We had what I later learned was a standard conversation between two recently separated people. I also learned that we were both "kickees" as apposed to "kickors". The club was made of "kickees". Let me explain. Usually when a married couple separates, one has already lined up a new partner. He or she is responsible for, and desires the separation. They are the "kickors". They don't join or participate in activities that are for unmarried's. On the other hand, "kickees" are interested in meeting other unmarried people. "Unmarried" as used here refers to people who have been married, as opposed to single people who have never been married. Many, or at least most start looking for that special person that does not have the personality problems of their former spouse. Problem often is, they think they meet that special one a number of times before they actually do Of course, there are a few old timers that gave up ever finding a new mate, but stay in the club awaiting some tender new meat. <u>Note; These are men and women.</u>

Now, getting to the standard conversation. "My husband (or wife) was a no good son of a bitch"`. This can be said in one sentence or it can be blown up into several paragraphs. Occasionally, but not very often, the "kickor" gets tired of being bothered for sex, and ends the marriage. The "kickee" from this relationship, if female, I learned to favor. They feel like they have been sexually starved and try to make up for it.

We left Denny's, got into my car, and I put an arm around her and gave her a kiss. Something was missing in that kiss. I asked if she would like to go to my house. The response was strong and loud, "I should say not!" Well I did not understand. Could be many reasons.

* * *

My older brother phoned and invited me to dinner. I asked if I could bring a friend. I thought about the women that I had met in the few weeks and sister-in-law. My brother had a masters degree. He worked as a public school psychologist. His wife was vice president of a large bank.

They lived in a dirty old house, built in 1906, in one of Los Angeles' wealthiest neighborhoods. She got a new Cadillac every year as part of her pay package. He was one of the world's greatest nature photographers. They were not Christians. I had spent many hours trying to get them to give their lives to Christ. They were good listeners; But they always finished each meeting with a feeling of sympathy for me for accepting all of this Christian stuff.

Which one do I take with me. Should I decide by looks? No. By sexual motivation? No. Formal education? No. Finally after many considerations I chose the one with a compatible occupation. That would be Valerie. Only a couple of hours with her at Denny's and she was not interested in going home with me. She was secretary to the CEO of one of the largest real estate developers in western United States.

The evening went well. We went out to a Chinese restaurant. I had guessed right, the ladies got along well. This was the first time I had seen my brother and his wife since before my split up. I received a lot of understanding on the telephone. William had said just phone him any time that I needed to talk. They were familiar with the many lovers that Bonnie had had, and all of the pain it had caused me. I had assured him that I was happy now. William was on his second marriage. His first was a shotgun marriage. He had two children by her. She was constantly cheating on him. Once I stayed all night with them. He got up and left for work at about six AM. I slept on the floor for lack of a second bed. I was 14 years old. His wife awakened me to ask if I would like to get in bed with her. I was tired of the hard floor, and quickly accepted. Once in bed I went to sleep quickly. She allowed me to sleep an hour pulled me close to her nude body. This was a new experience for me. I didn't know what to do, so I pretended to be sleeping. She knew that I was awake. She said, "If you will go to the mail box and get the mail, I will give you a nice piece of ass." I went and got the mail; But, I never got back in bed.

William's current wife is very different. She is the typical, "Nose up", conservative banker. William once told me that she liked sex. However she was very dry inside causing him to always use a lubricant which reduced the feeling for him.

The evening ended with hugs all around. William got me alone long enough to question my drinking. I had been the only one that ordered drinks before dinner.

June invited Valerie to come back anytime. I had chosen correctly. Valerie made a hit.

Driving toward our homes on the Hollywood Freeway, I asked Valerie, "Would you like to go to my house."

"I should say not !"

I took her home.

I drove in her drive way. Stopped. Looked at her; But, never touched. I said, " Would you like for me to walk you to the door."

"Yes, I would like that."

She unlocked the door, stepped in and to my surprise asked, "Would you like to come in."

With a kind of "Why bother" look on my face, "OK."

She led me to the living room, pointed to the couch and left the room. I sat down and waited about ten minutes. She had completely changed her cloths. She sat down beside me. I put both arms around her and kissed her. This was quiet different from our first kiss after leaving Denny's. It was warm and soft. I reached down and got hold of a breast out of curiosity. I said, "36C, right?" She didn't answer. I got the impression she didn't like my asking. I said, "36D ?". I suddenly became unhappy with the situation. I announced that I had to leave. She didn't walk me to the door. I drove away thinking about her. She was obviously intelligent, and very shy. Many women say, " You are the first since my ex-husband." In almost all cases, that is difficult to believe. In Valerie's case, I would have believed it. My best guess was she had to have sex at home because she used a diaphragm. She was about 32 years old and so still had use for birth control. If she had asked, I would have told her that I had a vasectomy.

I stopped at a liquor store and went home and got plastered.

I saw Valerie one more time.   That was a party at my house several months later. We said hello to each other and that was all.

Watching her that night, I developed the feeling that as she looked around at my house inside and out. She was say-

ing to herself look at all that I missed. I was a bit better off fi-nancially than most of the men in the club. Some times that gave me a slight advantage and some times just the opposite.

* * *

I was spending a quiet evening alone, except for my pint of Scotch whiskey. The phone rang. It was Steve Parker, my attorney friend. "Hello Steve, what is happening. I don't see you much."

"Everything in my life is great. I expect to be shipping out soon."

"Where are you going. That is, if you can say."

"I can't tell you precisely, but I can say, I am going to the land of Susie Wong. Kirk I have an unusual request to make of you. I have a 19 year old daughter who is a virgin. She is ready to start experiencing life. I am afraid that some young buck, that doesn't know what hc is doing will gct a hold of hcr and, wcll you know, mess her up. I want you to do the job."

My phone appeared to him to have gone dead. I was stunned. I had never had any one offer me anything before that shocked me like this did.

"Are you there Kirk."

"Yes, Steve, I am here."

"You are probably wondering why I chose you. I will tell you. You are my friend. You make out well with the young chicks. You are a decent, clean cut guy. That is why I want to entrust my daughter to you. Do you understand?"

"Yes Steve, I understand. When do you want me to meet her?"

He gave her good directions, she drove in the driveway an hour later

I opened the door and said, "hello Karen, please come in."

This was my first experience with a virgin. I was nervous. She seemed very relaxed, happy, smiling.

"Karen, have you had dinner?"

"Yes, I ate a couple of hours ago. But, don't let me stop you."

I didn't want to tell her, I was so nervous, I lost my appetite. "Would you like to go for a swim?"

"That sounds great, if you don't mind I don't have a bathing suit."

"I was hoping you did not have one."

This girl was beautiful.   She took off her cloths right in front of me, folding each piece, and placing them on a chair. Nude, she was even more beautiful. I had prepared for her arrival. All I was wearing was a pair of coveralls. I asked her to unzip them. Which she did without hesitation. She had to handle the zipper carefully when she got near the bottom because I had an erection. She worked the zipper around it with ease.

We both dove head first into the water. We each swam a little and then sat side by side on the love seat. I could not resist the temptation to feel her beautiful breasts just a little. She just smiled when I did.

I got out of the pool and said, "Stay there. I will be right back." I went in the outside door to the master bath, got a couple of large beach towels and returned. "The air is a little cool. I wanted her to wait for a towel. May I dry you", I asked.

"Please do."

"Let us go into the den. I want to have a little talk with you. I will sit across the room from you because I can't keep my hands off you when I sit too close. Do you understand?"

"Yes, I understand; but I like to have your hands on me."

"I want to know, do you just want to lose your virginity, or do you want to get an education in sex, and if so to what extent."

She looked me straight in the eyes and said, "I want to learn everything that you are capable of teaching me."

"You are 19 years old. If you can spend a few days with me, I will make you 39 years old in sexual knowledge."

"I have a few days."

"Stay there on the couch. I will spread my towel on the carpeting. I am going to hug and kiss you. **Relax** your body when I hug you. The first kiss will be with soft lips, lip to lip each time we kiss it will be wetter. The tongue will start being used on the third or fourth contact. Just a little at first, then a little more each time. The mouth on the first kiss is almost closed. At each kiss it opens more. As we get hotter the exchange of mouth fluids becomes greater. You will likely be able to tell by my actions if you are doing everything correctly. I will not say anything negative while we are embracing."

The hugs and kisses went exactly as I had prescribed. We were both hot.

"I am going to kiss, lick and suck on your breasts. Only you can tell the extent to which I can do this. Women vary a great deal on breast pleasure. Some like just a short kiss on the nipples. All can take licking all around the nipples. This gives most men pleasure. Most women like it. The sensitivity of the nipples varies a great deal from woman to woman. I have known a few that like me to chew on there nipples with my teeth."

The licking and sucking went well. The nipples liked it when I held them tightly between my lips while running my tongue back and forth on each.

"How Are you holding up?"

"I am having a ball. You should teach this in a class, Sex 131."

"Thank you. Now for the next part of Sex 131, you will be on your back on the towel. No not now. Listen first."

"OK."

"You are going to lay on your back, knees up, feet about two feet apart. I am going kiss your body all over from your face to the tip of your toes, then I will get between your legs, hold on to the outside of your legs and lick your clitoris, avoiding getting my tongue just below the clitoris where you urinate. OK if you understand, you can get on the towel now."

We both enjoyed this part of the teaching. I thought she wanted it to never end. She even held my head tightly against her clitoris.

"That was fabulous. I could stand that for hours", she said.

"I am happy that you liked it. We will go through every thing again tonight in bed. For now, I need a break. Lets get our cloths on and go to a restaurant a few blocks away and have something to eat."

"Will you snap my bra ?"

Karen and I got to know a lot about each other as we consumed our meals. I learned she is a full time student at UCLA. She asked how many women I have sex with. I told her, "Not very many."

She just smiled.

Back at the house, in the den again, she asked, "Are we going to go to bed."

"Not yet. We still have some class time. No, don't take your clothes off. For the next lesson, you will be fully dressed. Remain seated on the couch. You are going to suck on me. Commonly known as a blow job. Pull your upper lip in to cover your upper teeth. Put your tongue slightly out of your mouth to cover your lower teeth. Now unzip my pants, take out my prick and hold your hand in a position that will limit how much of my prick goes in your mouth. You have probably heard of Deep Throat, a movie years ago. Sometime you should try that, that is remove your hand and put the whole thing down your throat. But, first, don't just quickly put it in your mouth like you want to get it out of sight. Look at it. Touch it. Kiss it. Lick it. And most of all smile, and enjoy everything that you are doing"

"Do you want me to blow you now?"

"Right now."

She followed my instructions perfectly. "You did great. I almost ejaculated in your mouth. That is something we can do later. Now, student choice. What would you like to do. Go for a swim? Have a mixed drink? Retire for the evening? Or what?"

"I would like to go to bed for the evening, But, not to retire."

"OK, lets brush our teeth, take a shower together, and go to bed."

I washed her between her legs saying, "I don't want to get a mouth full of soap when I eat you (lick her clitoris) so I'll hold the shower head down here to rinse you well."

In bed I could feel the heat radiating from her body as she pressed against me. We kissed several times. Each a little wetter and a little more tongue than the preceding. I sucked, and licked, and kissed her body all over. The same as she did to me. I turned around, moving my head closer to the foot of the king sized bed. Gently, I grasped her legs and rolled us both over ending with me on my back and her on top of me. She suddenly realized that my prick was looking up at her. She touched it, licked and kissed it before putting it in her mouth and sucking for what seemed like hours. Much to my surprise, she suddenly pulled it out of her mouth to avoid biting it as she climaxed. "You did well for a beginner."

I moved back up facing her. She was panting and I could see beads of sweat on her fore head. She said, "That was ——Wow."

I tried kissing her; But, She could only give short kisses because she needed her mouth open for breathing. I was hoping her heart beat and breathing would slow. I could see the news paper, "19 year old girl dies of heart attack in bed." And I am telling the police, "It was accident, I fucked her to death."

The next morning I was in the kitchen making coffee when she walked in wearing just a sweater of mine. She gave me a little kiss on the cheek and said, "Good morning professor."

"You didn't get here until late yesterday afternoon. Are you prepared for a full day of class today?"

She smiled and said, "Let's get started."

"Do you want to go out to breakfast or eat here."

"If we went out, it would take away time from our class. So let's eat here."

After breakfast, I gave her the master bath and I took one of the others. I said, "We will each take care of our own business and shower."

I spent the next two days teaching her the various flavors of jelly that I put on my penis before she sucks it, how she, with me on my back, goes under my balls and sticks her tongue in my rectum. We covered 12 different positions for intercourse. During the first position, I put my penis in her for the first time. That is what she came for. "You lost your virginity. I hope you enjoyed the teaching. Come back occasionally for a brush up. What are you going to tell your father?"

"I will tell him that I had a wonderful time. I feel like I have 20 years of sexual experience that I received in three days."

"And now what is your attitude toward sex."

"I think it is the most outstanding thing humans can do."

"Give me a big kiss. That is your tuition. If you have any virgin girl friends that are a good looking as you, and need SEX-131, give them my number."

* * *

Erna was Jewish, by choice. Not by birth. She was widowed in Germany. Her husband died of cancer. She had had a happy love life with him. Her only child, a daughter, was seven years old. Erna was 32, had a nice figure. She spoke English with a heavy German accent. Jewish by choice came about as a little girl, hearing the stories from older people, many of whom had been in concentration camps. She developed a hateful attitude toward Germans who were not Jewish, and so converted to Judaism.

I met Erna at a **PWS** group discussion that I was moderating. The subject was, *Interfaith dating and marriage.* At the conclusion of the formal discussion about ten people gathered around to talk personally.

One Jewish man told me of a white, Jewish friend having a successful marriage to a black Baptist. All of the conversation, and I mean all, agreed that inter-faith dating and marriage were perfectly acceptable.

After a few years to observe the subject, I learned that dating the opposite, as I previously mentioned, holds true with religious difference. But when it came to marriage, op-posites was no longer desired. Jews married Jews, gentiles married gentiles, and born again Christians were willing to wait years to find another Christian.

"I liked the program tonight. You must have done this for a long time. Leading such a group. You did good." In a thick German accent.

"Thank you for the compliment. I have only a few months of experience. Are you a new member? I don't remember having seen you before."

"I am not a member. A friend told me about this meeting tonight."

"I will be moderating a similar group three nights from tonight. The subject will be, "*extra mari-tal sex*". I hope you will come."

Three nights later I got to the host house a lit-tle early. I set up the chairs just the way I wanted them. One chair beside me I put a sign on that called out, 'RESERVED'. When the word sex was in the title of the group discussion, the crowd was larger. I think that I was finally getting close to the point of admitting that sex is free among unmarried adults even though few admit it.

The crowd was gathering. Erna had not appeared as yet. However I felt sure that she would.

Time to start, "Welcome to **PWS**. There will be no bilateral conversation. Please give us your answers. Don't direct statements or questions to another person. Tonight we are going to discuss *"extra marital sex"*. We will not be limited by age. That is some of you have teen age and pre teen age children. I hope you will learn something here tonight that will help you to understand what you and your children are facing. We will discuss older divorced and widowed people. That is enough introduction. Hold it, Erna, came in, I saved a chair for you right here. Now for starters, What would you tell your neighbor if she advised you that her daughter had been taking her birth control pills and replacing them with aspirin ?"

The hands went up. About half way through the program a woman I did not recognize said "I am shocked by the number of women that speak so openly about sex as though they were offering their bodies."

"You must be new to **PWS.** What is your name?"

She said "Jane."

I replied by asking, "All of you women in the group raise your hands to show that you make sex easy for men. Not one hand went up."

One more question, I asked, "How many of you men actively peruse sex with ladies on the first, second or third date?"

Not one hand went up. "Jane, You must have some other club in mind, not **PWS.**"

Generally at **PWS** group discussions the moderator speaks very little. But, I decided to spice up the discussion, "One of the universities along with the National Institutes of Health gives us the information that among men in the 75 to 85 age group 40 percent are still sexually active. Women in the same age group are only 17 percent active. Those in excellent health were almost twice as likely to be interested in sex as those in poor health. So if you are interested in maintaining your sexual activity watch your diet and exercise regularly."

Clair and I drew the largest crowds. The subjects were always something to do with sex. One night I moderated, "*All about sex.*" That brought the largest group ever.

* * *

I invited Erna to my house the next day for a swim and lunch. When she arrived she said, "I brought my daughter for protection."

"That is fine, I love children. And how old are you, I asked the young lady?

" I am 7."

"Do you like to swim?"

"Yes."

We enjoyed the day. The next time that I moderated, Erna was there. She went home with me. In the bed she stuck her name tag to the head of the bed and said, "Now that I have been initiated I guess I should join the club."

She had a position when having sex that annoyed me. With me on top, she would have her legs aiming straight up in the air.

When we were dressed and sitting back in the living room, she started talking about her past, She said, " I worked in New York City before moving to Los Angeles. There I only worked from 9 to 5 with an hour for lunch". In the Los Angeles area she was not paid for her lunch period.

Erna lived in a rented apartment that was on my way to and from the place where I was working. So one day I stopped. She seemed very happy to see me. She offered something to eat and asked what I like t drink.

"Scotch", I said.

"Tomorrow when you stop, I will have scotch for you."

I turned down the offer of food, and bid her good night. As I drove away, I thought, how presumption of her to assume that I would stop tomorrow.

She was right. The next night, I stopped.

She gave me a kiss. I took a comfortable seat.

"What would you like with the scotch? Water? Soda?"

"Nothing. Just straight"

She sat on the floor next to my chair and started rubbing my leg above the knee. She noticed that I had finished my drink. She quickly stopped rubbing, jumped up and got a refill. She got back on the floor: But on her knees this time, and directly in front of me. She started unzipping my pants.

She looked up and asked, "OK?"

In just nodded.

She sucked hard, like she knew what she was doing. The scotch slowed me down. I think she realized this would be the result of the scotch. So she worked long and hard to get me to climax.

I returned two or three times a week for about two months. Then we discussed her living with me in my house. Her daughter thought that would be great. We worked out an agreement that was appealing to both of us. She would have no rent to pay and I would have no food to buy.

This is an arrangement that many couples like. Personally, I believe that it is immoral and generally a bad idea for young single couples to cohabitate. The beauty of getting married in a religious environment is lost. Having God's blessing on a marriage is important. ....What God has joined together, let no man put under.... Forsaking all others until death.... During the great depression of the 1930s divorces were few. Since world war two they have been high. It is safe to say that what is happening today, the opposite will happen later. Older divorced and widowed people are different. The divorce rate of second marriages is considerably higher than for first marriages. The divorce rate for third marriages is lower than first or second marriages. Why do so many people get divorced? Many reasons are given. Many reasons are suspected. However most of these reasons are wrong. In almost all cases the kicker has found someone else. The movie industry and even television ads promote sex. When I was a teen age boy my buddy and I traveled 20 miles to see a movie with the silhouette of a nude woman behind obscure glass. For quite some time children have been able to see far more at the cinema or on television. Sex is played as a thrilling and wonderful thing. **It is for some. It is not for others.** *For me it is. For my wife, it was not. I learned that the reason for her many escapades was that see was trying to find wonderful, happy sex. After six failed marriages, I believe she finally gave up and married a Marine officer who is a devout Christian. We can't change ourselves. We can't change others. What is the answer then,* **"Acceptance".** *We learn to accept ourselves and those around us.*

* * *

Another **PWS** party at my house. About 170 in attendance. My house was on top of a hill. The back yard looked all the way across the San Fernando valley. The pool light was the only light in the back yard. This made the yard look romantic. A five piece band played in the grand room. The room was paneled and had a sphere, covered with chipped glass rotating.

It interested me that there were two black men and two black women. Never once that evening did I see them together. The women stayed in one end of the house and the men stayed at the opposite end of the house. About ten

*Mexicans were among the guests. I estimated the group was at least 50 % Jewish. These people were here to meet some one of the opposite sex. Note, I said opposite. One thing I never met in **PWS** was a homo sexual. Most of the people wanted to meet some one different. different from their ex-spouse, different size, shape, color, just different.*

Clair was there, busy as ever. She was in charge. Being in charge of a party with 170 people was a big job.

As I wondered through the crowed, I spotted the beautiful young woman with the raven hair that I had seen at the general meeting. When I was about four feet away, she suddenly looked up at me. I was unable to speak. I just stood there looking at her. I reached with both of my hands at the same time. She did the same thing. I let go of one hand and walked with her to a quiet place in the back yard. We sat on two chaise lounges and held hands. Finally she spoke for the first time, "My name is Andrea".

"I am Kirk. I can't explain the feeling, what you do to me."

With tears running down her cheeks, "I have never before had a man affect me like this ."

Maybe for the first time in my life, I feel a relationship between love and sex. Sex to me has been fun.

It was necessary to get rid of that feeling like someone had forced something up my rectum. The sex that I have had in the past few weeks was like one might have with a prostitute. That is good feeling, lots of relief; But, I could walk away from it with no emotional attachment. This young lady had plenty of sex appeal. She had a perfect figure, or maybe five pounds over weight, and I felt like I would like to spend hours in bed with her.

I asked, "Where do you live or better still tell me all about yourself."

"I am 25 years old, divorced, two children, one boy and one girl, I have an apartment in North Hollywood. I am Islamic, from upstate New York. Now tell me about your self."

"I am 36, divorced or almost that is, two children, one boy, one girl, I have custody, I am a Christian, I live right here."

"You mean this is your house?"

"Not only the house, but the yard too."

"Where are the children?"

"My daughter is away at school, high school that is, my son is about two blocks away spending the

night with a son of one of the **PWS** members. I have
been separated less than two months. I filed a non-
contested divorce

Six weeks ago. Where are your children?”

“ With my parents. They live next door to me.”

“I have to hang around until the party is over, or
almost over.   Then could we go to a restaurant?”

“ Yes, lets do.”

A handsome young Italian man seemed to be
eyeing up Erna. A couple of times I noticed they
were at a location in the back yard by them selves.

Having a party at my house, I thought would be
a pleasure. It turned out to be a curse. All of the
parties involved each man bring a bottle of liquor.
There were many bottles, partially filled, left after
each party. My drinking got worse to where I was
drunk three or four time a week. A good thing was
normally at each party a few women would leave
dishes or sweaters as an excuse to come back later
to pick them up. Lots of sex and no liquor would
have been a more healthful life. I had a lot of
both. What a fool I was. With a hang over most
Sunday mornings, my church attendance went
down.

I have thought many times about assets that I had and whether they effected my ability to attract females. After months to thinking about it, I decided it was not an effect for the general female population. How ever my assets did effect a certain type. For example, a woman that had never been well off financially and/or was living in a small apartment would be attracted to my home. One that had already had a nice big, house or a husband that had an upper class income would not be attracted to me because of my home. My new Cadillac, I don't believe it was an asset in getting any lady. My looks; Well, if I was ugly enough to scare people away, I think that would be a factor. I developed some male friendships that had old cars, little apartments and were anything from ugly to very good looking. We all did about the same with the ladies, except for one difference. My ability to do public speaking and lead various groups were assets, I believe.

Andrea and I went in my car to a restaurant as soon as people started leaving. We held hands most of the time in the restaurant. We talked about her employment and mine. My employment was a definite disadvantage to a marriage with children. Because I worked short term jobs that were anywhere in the world. My own children were old enough that they could attend boarding school.

Two nights later I went to her apartment just to learn that Monday nights she was in *Powers Modeling School*. I left a note and we got together Tuesday night for volley ball with the club. After, I asked if she was ready to go home and she said, "I am ready to go anywhere that you want to take me."

I passed up a nice looking bed partner. However, I got a date to take her to the Rose Bowl, Friday night to see Johnny Cash. Understand; This was rare for me to have a "date" with any girl. Just having parties at my house supplied more females than I could ever keep up with.

After the show we went to my house for the most satisfying sex I have ever had. She said it was the first time she had ever climaxed three times in one evening. One of those was while she was blowing me. She spent the night and we went back at it the next morning.

Driving to her place, I commented, "that was great sex we had".

"I thought so too".

"You said that you were Islamic. Does that mean you live by the Koran? "

"Yes, I do."

"Does that mean that you can have sex outside of marriage?"

"I will have to admit, that is a little bit question-able. Do you know anything about the Koran?"

"Very little."

"Some time, if we ever see each other again, I will enlighten you about Islam."

"What do you mean, if we ever see each other again? An army couldn't keep me away from you."
We saw each other three to four times a week. I met her parents and her two children. Her father was a quiet man. Her mother spoke enough for both of them. Andrea had told her that I was a Christian. That seem to be a concern for her. Her children took after their grand parents, quiet son, vociferous daughter.

Erna and her daughter moved out. The reason given was that in New York, she had a married man that was having problems with his wife take her out almost every time he was in town. When he did not have time he would leave $20 on the table for her when he left in the mornings. "What do you do for me? You take me to group discussions." I didn't say anything; But I was thinking she was a prostitute.

One evening as Andrea and I were sitting alone in my living room (one of those rare times when we were not in bed) we had difficulty keeping our hands off each other. She asked, "How serious are you about Christianity?"

"Very! That is the most important thing in my life."

"Well, I am going to tell you a few things about my religion. It has been very misunderstood because of a few trouble makers. OK?"

"Muhammad wrote the Koran in the year 622. It gives us guidelines to live by including love, sex, and mostly about family. Man and wife have equal responsibility to give to the other sexual satisfaction. They each have equal rights to divorce if sexual pleasure is not provided by the partner. However it is easier for a man to divorce a woman than for a woman to divorce a man. He has only to say, I divorce you three times. A man can have four wives maximum. However there have been many exceptions. In fact Muhammad exceeded that number himself. A man that had several wives would keep them all together in a part of the house where they would not bother him. He would trust a eunuch to watch over them. Muhammad's foot prints are in the Rock of Mariah, from which he ascended into heaven."

"That is very interesting. Thank you."

My church had a party at my house two weeks later. I had Andrea as my hostess. This was a little shocking to a few people, my having a girl friend so soon after separating from my wife. However as news travels fast in a church, most knew that Bonnie had been committing adultery. If I had told men in that church about all of the available women in the unmarried world, I don't believe they would believe me.

I received a phone call from a man in another chapter of **PWS**. He wanted to have a party at my house. Some organization to which he held membership wants to have a special party that would be all nude. They would bring some kind of special lotion too rub each others backs. The attendees are all vegetarians. They put health above most every thing in life. They would like to have the pool water above 85 degrees.

I asked, "How many people?"

He said, "12 to 15 men and the same for women."

"What is the likelihood of them becoming sexually involved?"

"I suppose it could happen.", he said.

I gave my OK. The group started showing up at about 5:30. When the doorbell rang, I was in the pool, nude. I opened the front door about one inch. A lovely lady about 25 years old stood there.

I said, "What can I do for you."

"I am sorry. I was told that there was to be a party here at seven o'clock. I don't have a car. A friend was coming this way and gave me a ride."

"That is enough. You have the right house. My problem is I don't have any clothes on. If you want to give me a few minutes I'll get dressed."

"That is not necessary. I don't mind if you don't have any cloths on."

I swung the door open and in she came.

I said, "Make yourself at home. I am going back in the pool."

She followed me to the pool and said. "You mind if I join you."

"Not at all. Come in."

I could see thru the sliding glass door taking off her cloths.

When she got to the pool she said, "I don't want to get my hair wet."

"Sit down here on the love seat with me. I prom-ise to not wet your hair."

As soon as she was seated, I put one hand on her upper leg. She didn't indicate that she cared. I asked her a few questions about the club. She indicated that the club was for people who were lacking in sexual motivation. Some or most had had bad experiences with sex. That gave me an idea. I took one of her hands and put it on my penis. She looked scared. But she did not move her hand and she did not say anything. Some females, especially less than good looking ones would be terribly insulted, would pull away, get out of the pool, maybe even demand an apology. Good looking ones likely would squeeze it a little and inquire as to what my intentions were. This girl was good looking; But she didn't fit either group.

I guess she was a member of a third group, i.e., afraid of sex.

We sat and talked. I knew that if I made a play for her, she may say "yes" or she may say "no". But either way, she would not be worth the effort.

The crowed gathered. 12 men and 13 women. They brought a couple of bottles of wine and some kind of chips. They spread large towels on the carpeting of the den, living room, and master bed room. The leader of the group announced, "I am going into the bed room and remove my clothing."

The others stood around and talked. A few kissed. The leader came into the room wearing a robe. He went out, dropped his robe near the pool, and jumped in. They all followed. In about ten minutes they were all in the water, nude. I took off my cloths that I had just put on, and joined them.

A few at a time, they left the pool and went back into the house. I was the last one out. I went in the living room, the den, and the master bed room. I did not see any one being rubbed with Lotion. In each room a woman lay on her back while the men took turns laying on her. I suppose the women took turns being the one laying on the back. I didn't stick around to find out. One woman stood in the hall by herself. She was a little bit older than the rest, very nice looking, large breasts that didn't need anything supporting them.

I went back into the pool. Soon the women, one at a time, came back into the pool just to talk to me. Each one said, "come in the house and join in the fun."

I paid no attention. Why? I don't know. This was my first encounter with group sex. To me, sex was a personal thing. It was not something that I would do for an audience.

A few days later, I received a letter from the big breasted, slightly older woman that had been standing in the hall. She apologized for having not motivated me. She also explained that her husband had dropped her off for the activity. Well, I thought, it takes all kinds.

* * *

I had just finished cleaning the swimming pool when my phone rang.

"Hello, Kirk?"

"Yes."

"This is Wanda. I met you at the **PWS** party at your house."

"Yes Wanda, so well I remember. How are you?"

"I just had some spare time to talk so I decided I wanted to talk to you."

"Well, I don't like to talk on the phone. Can you come up here?" This was a bit of chicanery just to get her where I could see her.

"Do you remember how to get here?"

"Yes. "No problem."

The PWS party had a few first time women. I had hardly noticed because of meeting Andrea. And I lied, I didn't remember Wanda.

She arrived about 20 minutes later. Very good looking she was. Blonde, about five feet four inches, and likely about 120 pounds. She was wearing a conservative white blouse that buttoned in the front, white peddle pushers, and sandals. I noticed the beautiful feet, nicely tanned.

I invited her into the living room where she chose to sit on a sofa. I wondered if she expected me to sit next to her. I sat across the room.

"Would you like a beer or something else?"

"A beer sounds nice."

"There you are." As I handed it to her and walked across the room and took my seat.

She drank that beer down so fast that I asked, "Would you like another?"

"No. It only takes one ."

What she said along with the way she looked at me left no question. I walked across the room, got down on my knees, and kissed her legs. "Do you want to try the bed room?"

"Let's go," she said

She was removing her clothes as she walked into the room. I interrupted her long enough for a short, juicy kiss. Short because she was in a hurry.

As I was learning about the sexual motivation of the female, with few exceptions the better looking they are the higher is their motivation. The reason is from the time they develop a woman's figure they are sought after. This is generally true. However I know one exception. A skinny, not good looking girl with sores and pock marks on her face left her husband. He was a nice looking guy that would have no problem lining up bed partners. But he didn't need to. Each day between five and six PM his ugly wife would show up at his door. About an hour to an hour and a half later she would leave him again. Horny and ugly is very bad combination.

Wanda was a little bit of a surprise. As I lay on my back, she kissed me on the lips the chest the legs; but, Not on the penis. She got on top of me and rubbed her breasts back and forth across my face. She reached down and guided my penis in, then kicked both of her knees up on the sides of my chest. Soon she climaxed. She then pulled out, turned around, sat on my chest while she washed my penis with a wash cloth and a pan of water. Then she started sucking on it. Then she put it back in. In and out, she worked it for about five to ten minutes. Next she pulled it out and washed it again.

And then back into her, facing away from my face. She repeated this between her legs, out and wash it, suck it routine about ten times. Then she pushed and pulled side to side until I moved with her. Then one big roll until she was on the bottom and I was on top. I could not figure out how she did that without it coming out. While finally, I was in the driver's seat, I did some sucking on the breasts.

Acceptance of sucking on breasts as I mentioned before, is something that varies from woman to woman. Type one; Only accepts during intercourse, otherwise go very easy. Type two; Allows sucking any time. However during intercourse chewing with varying force of a man's teeth is desired. Type three; Very little licking or sucking during pre play. After it is in (usually with her on top) they like to have her nipples pinched and rubbed against a man's beard.

I went lip to lip with her, open mouths, we climaxed together.

This gal must have had two PhD's in sexual performance. If she wanted to sell it, I am sure she could get $1,000 for a performance.

* * *

The wife of a family that I went to church with phoned me to explain how a neighbor of theirs husband left her a couple of weeks ago. They described her as, "a lovely lady, just a little over weight. She is lonely and if you had time maybe you two could get together."

"Do you want me to call her or is she to phone me?"

"Oh no, she would never phone you. I will give you her phone number."

I invited her up to my house for a dinner. She agreed to bring a salad.

That evening she arrived for dinner. I had been told that she was a little over weight. That was a gross under statement. She was sloppy fat. She was definitely not good looking. Don't get me wrong, I have known some fat women with beautiful complexions that were very appealing. Their meat was well proportioned, that is they carried their weight well. But, I had her for dinner and I would make the best of it. We had the usual conversation how many children, type of work, etc. That only opened the way for the usual story about how good she had been in the marriage and what a son of a bitch her husband had been. I felt like stopping her and telling her that I had already heard the story. I thought a lot about it then finally asked her, "Did you give your husband sexual satisfaction ?"

"I am shocked that you would ask me such a question. But since you asked, I will answer. We were married for 20 years, had two children. While I was pregnant with the second one, we stopped having sex. He thought we should continue having sex. He never could explain why. I was good to him. I loved him. I still love him."

Tears started running down her face. I reached over and started to hold her hands. She quickly pulled away, saying, "Don't touch me. You men are all alike. Sex on the brain."

"I didn't have sex on my brain when I tried to hold your hands."

" I am afraid to be here alone with you. "

"Why ? "

"All of my life, I have read about women and girls being raped when they were alone with men."

"And I seem like the sort of man that would do that to you ?", I asked.

"All men are like that."

"I want you to leave. I want you to ask our mutual friend that gave your phone number to me, what kind of guy I am. Ask if I am the sort of person that would rape any woman. She and her husband know me well. They were both in a bible class that I taught. They are well acquainted with my x-wife and what I went through with her sexual escapades. Look in the mirror when you get home. Ask yourself if you are so beautiful that any man getting alone with you would have only sex on his mind. Join a group for unmarried people. Get into a bible study group. Go out with men. Have men over for dinner. And I will bet you now that you will seldom ever find any man that will pursue you sexually. Don't forget the dish that the salad was in."

* * *

Wanda phoned to invite me to her house for the afternoon. I accepted, but I had to get out of a previous invitation from Andrea. Andrea was my number one girlfriend. However, I felt like I just had to spend a little more time with Wanda. I didn't think of my relationship with her as long term. My relationship with Andrea I thought could lead to marriage.

*I guess I was like just about everyone else, I wanted to play, have some excitement, for a while and **then settle back down**. But what about settling down with another woman like Bonnie? Seems like almost every woman that I have met or heard about from my male friends is quick and anxious to get sexually involved. Was I to believe that after the ring was on the finger they would not get involved* *with anyone else? I used to believe that cold women were more likely to cheat than hot ones because they were always looking for satisfaction. In fact this describes my Bonnie. Sex to her was to be exciting. With a stranger it is more likely to be exciting as she wonders what is he going to do next. A really warm woman in particular a Christian gets more out of sex with her husband as the years go by. Maybe it is a good time to mention who is hot, cold, and just right. I have met hundreds of both males and females. Almost all considered them selves, "just right".*

If one had a partner that wanted sex more often then they, the partner was obviously oversexed. If less often, well they had a problem also. I remember defending one of my buddies. I estimate that he had sex with about 100 different women a year. He was healthy, had plenty of spare time, and his problem wasn't a problem. He really enjoyed sex. He never talked marriage. According to the reports that women gave me, He was a very good sex partner. But the stories were always going around that he was crazy, had a one tract mine. Women who were new to the club, I think, were all warned to stay away from him. Do you want to guess what that did for him? They flocked to him. He never kept secret about his affairs. He reported all of the details to me and his other male friends

* * *

I didn't know what to tell Andrea. Probably something to do with my children. I assured her that I loved her and was looking forward to spending a lot of time with her the next day.

Wanda lived in a simple little house (about 1700 square feet). That surprised me because her x was a busy attorney. She introduced me to her three daughters, ages 6, 8,and 10. She quietly told me to stay away from her daughters. We took them to a cinema in my car. Just as soon as Wanda got back in the car she cuddled up close to me. I planted a big wet kiss on her. Instantly I felt a bulge in my slacks. Before I got out of the parking lot she was trying to unzip me. I stopped long enough to accommodate her. Good thing I remembered how to get to her house because she never looked up. When we arrived on her driveway, she took it out of her mouth, smiled, and just said, "Come in".

I had to make a joke, " Do you mean cum in your mouth ?"

"Would you like a drink first?"

"Yes I'll have a glass of whiskey."

I suggested that we start the show in the living room. She agreed. She sat down on the couch with all of her cloths on. I stood in front of her, unzipped my slacks took it out and she grabbed it.

I said, "Not yet. Hold your lips almost closed, just slightly open. That is just right."

I remembered seeing many pictures of women advertising lipstick with their lips slightly open.

I took it in my own hand and rubbed it back and forth across her lips. Then I asked her, "Open your lips now I am gong to put it in." I provided the motion, in and out for about fifteen minutes. I was about to climax.

I felt it coming on. Soon, I knew. I would try to relax to put it off. Then finally just as I started to shoot that stuff into her mouth, I pulled it out and shot it all across her face. Her mouth was still open so I put it back in because that is the time when I get the most feeling.

After she washed her face we each had a drink. I put my penis back in my slacks and zipped up. She walked over to me fully dressed and said, "Kirk that was wonderful. I never had that before."

"I thought you would like it. Glad you did."

I danced her to the middle of the room, then pushed her lightly. She laid down on the floor (fully clothed). I unbuckled her belt and pulled off her slacks and her under panties. First time I noticed what a beautiful pair of legs she had. I got on the floor on my stomach between her legs, pulled her knees up and spread, feet on the floor..

Her phone rang. She said, "Just a moment"

She waited until the answering machine came on, and a man's voice started speaking. "That son of a bitch" as she jumped to her feet and ran to the phone. "I told you before, I am not an attorney, I can't negotiate with you."

It was obviously her x-husband. I could not understand why she had to speak then. Why couldn't she call him back later or wait for his next call. I walked to the phone gave her a short kiss on the cheek and walked out. I could still hear her yelling at him when I got to my car.

While driving, I was thinking what one of my Jewish buddies said, "*The way to make a Jewish girl stop fucking. Marry her.*"

* * *

I went home, took a shower and sat by the pool. I was still a little shook up after that visit with Wanda. I only sat there about 10 minutes when the phone rang. Shall I answer it or not ? I let it ring about ten times before I got up and answered it. "Andrea, How are you my love ? Yes I got things squared away, and was just relaxing by the pool, thinking about you."

"I'm horny. The kids are at my parents apartment and"

"Stop right there. Your place or mine?"

"Yours"

"We will make love for an hour then go out to dinner. Maybe you should bring a second outfit with you. The first one must be easy for me to remove, and a second one is for going out to dinner."

"I'll be there in 20 minutes."

I asked myself, "How could I even look at another woman?"

Twenty minutes later the door bell rang. I opened it just a crack to see if it was she. Because I was wearing nothing. "Come in Andrea".

She looked me up and down. First time she had seen me nude in the light.

"You look like you are ready for action."

"I am ready to put my arms around you and hold you tightly."

"Where may I put my robe?", She asked.

"Is that a robe? I thought it was a coat. Put it in the bedroom."

"Come with me. I want to be sure to put it in the right place."

She walked into the bedroom. I followed closely. She turned around and said, "Stand right there." She made a show of removing the rob. Slowly, gradually it uncovered her. Soon I could see she was wearing little or nothing under it. When it was completely off she was nude.

"May I move toward you know?"

"You will only be able to get within a foot or so because that stiff thing sticking out in front will stop you."

CHAPTER 10

I took Andrea to the airport. She had to fly to New York to tend to a sick aunt. She said she would be gone a week or two. I saw her to the gate, waited for time to board, than kissed her good bye. We assured each other of our mutual love. She had tears running down that beautiful face as she walked away.

A **PWS** party had already been scheduled for my house for that night. I hurried directly home. Clair was already there with her crew of workers. She had a key to my house for just such occasions.

We had about two hours before they would start arriving. I spent one hour of that time in the swimming pool. I dried myself off and went to my bed room to get dressed. I just got my swim trunks off when my bed room door opened. It was Clair.

"Seeing you in your birthday suit is enough to make me forget the reason I came."

"It has been a few months. Do you have enough time for a renewal ?"

"Let me go talk to the ladies to make sure they don't decide to need me."

I laid on my back and waited for Clair's return. This was rather handy when we are short of time. She will not need to remove any clothing that is if she is still having female problems, she uses only her mouth.

She entered the room. Took one look at me, didn't remove any clothing. Just laid down beside me with her lips next to my hip. I rolled over facing her. She put it in her mouth and I started pumping.

People were showing up like a herd. Looked like we may top 200. Harold Morris and Joyce Axle came together, April made a showing and offered to help.

I called her aside and whispered in her ear, " You could help by staying after all of the others leave and going to bed with me and having wild sex until the sun comes up."

"I know you are kidding Kirk. I wish I could do just what you just requested. But you know, I can't."

The party got into full swing. I started each party by playing a phonograph record, '*Louis Pima, Wonderland by Night*'. I went into the living room and some one was sitting in my chair. I pointed and another person told him that he could sit anywhere in the house except in that chair.

When I told Andrea that I loved her, I believed I was sincere. But I couldn't help looking around the house at all of the beautiful young ladies. All divorced or widowed. All looking for a love affair. Most looking for something to hold on to. Almost all are ready to hit the bed with someone that they will meet tonight.

I wondered all over the house. I think most people believed that I was acting as a security guard. Actually, I was looking at the new crop of females. Not bad, I thought. I walked into the den and found a real beauty. About 5 feet 8 inches, I guess 140 pounds, black hair, and a beautiful complication.

I introduced myself as did she. She had her back to me and started leaning forward to look at something near the floor. I put one hand on each hip to give her support. She quickly rose, turned around and said, "Don't handle me".

"I am sorry. I was not trying to get fresh. I just thought you could get a closer look with a little support".

She turned around and looked me straight in the eyes. I was confused. I had developed the belief that a woman's mouth could say anything but her **eyes would always tell the truth**. Her eyes were telling me that she was very warm. I reached up and put a hand on a shoulder. She quickly shrugged it off. At that point, I decided to go back to wondering through the house.

I said, "I hope you enjoy the party", as I walked away.

I met a very shapely Negro, African American, black or whatever the current acceptable description is. I have a solution to that problem, I.E. outlaw same race marriage. After a few generations we would all be the same color. I met her in the kitchen. She was very attractive.

She said, "Wow, would I like to cook in this kitchen."

"Some time maybe I will give you a chance to do that."

"What do you mean, You will give me a chance? Is this your house?"

"Yes. My name is Kirk, and you are?"

"Lynda. With a 'Y'."

I learned that she was an accountant where I was working, and a professional singer. I got her phone number, excused myself and went back to making my rounds.

Buck and Len were standing in the foyer where they could get early shots at the females as they arrive, I extended a hand and said, "Why do you guys work so hard when you know it would be difficult to not win a lady for the night ?"

Len spoke with Buck nodding agreement, "Kirk, you have it made, the fancy house, the new Cadillac, and most of all, your ability to spread the bull shit at all of your group discussions."

"Do you not think that what I say when I moderate helps you?"

Buck spoke up quickly, "Len, Kirk does tell the women that it is OK."

"Listen Kirk, do you have a hostess tonight?" Len asked.

"No."

"I want you to play the game a bit more fairly. Tonight I want you to have a girl stay after the party. I mean one that you never knew before. She hits the sack with you and you tell us tomorrow how good it was."

"Let us shake on that." I knew that at least 80% of the women here where available, ready and willing.

I spotted a nice looking girl across the room. I recognized her as one that Buck had already had. He, like most of the men in **PWS**, told his buddies all about his sexual experiences. As I walked across the room, I thought what approach should I use ? I decided to first ask her to dance. Then rather than use my usual, any approach except the direct approach, I would just hit it directly.

"Would you like to dance?"

"Thank you for asking. I would love to dance."

I immediately held her closely with one leg pressing between her legs.

Then I whispered in her ear, "I would sure like to give you a good fucking tonight."

She suddenly pushed away, saying, "I don't believe my ears."

*I thought, she is playing the game. She likes a little
bull, two or three dances, and then ask her to stay after the
others had left. This causes her to believe that she has met
a gentleman, a guy that has respect for her, not someone
who is after just any sex partner. Most women are this way
when they are first let out into the unmarried world. Then
if they don't meet a guy to marry or live with or at least go
steady with, they stop playing that game. Which is more
honest?*

My second target was one that I had seen at **PWS**
functions for all of the time that I had been in the
club. Above average looking, a little on the thin side,
but with sizable busts. "Would you like to dance?"

*Getting dance partners was easy because the women out-
numbered the men about two to one at parties and all other
club functions except volleyball. I have asked many men to
come as guests to some of the activities and usually they refused. Why? The most common reason given was they had
other things to do, such as hunting, fishing, athletic events.
The second most common reason was they felt that California
courts and their wives had robbed them in the divorce actions.
They were still heterosexual but would just live without.*

I held my second target closely with my leg posi-
tioned the same as with the first one. Then I popped

the question, "How would you like to stay after the crowed leaves, go to bed with me and get a good fucking?"

She answered, "Kirk, I would love to any night except tonight. Three of us girls came together. I drove. How about tomorrow night?"

I took a little break and walked around the house. First I passed Len and Buck. They looked my way without interrupting their conversations with their marks for the night. I winked as I passed. The house was wall to wall people. I caught one woman putting out a cigarette on my vinyl floor. I reported her to Clair who promptly escorted her to the front door.

My third victim for the night was Doreen, the girlfriend of Steve Parker who was in Hawaii. Also was known as Doctor Parker. Think of John Wayne and you have this guy. He had a doctor of law, a black belt in judo, and worked for the CIA. I got letters and cards from him from all over the world. His attitude toward women was, *'there are plenty to go around'*. I know that he would have no objection to me playing with his girlfriend while he was gone. In fact, I will tell him all about it, if it works out, the next time I see him. He was as generous with his girlfriend as he was with his daughter.

"You look like a lady waiting for someone to grab you by the hand and pull you out on the dance floor."

"You have that right."

As we danced, I never held her closely as I had the others. I looked down at her after a few minutes. She looked up with inviting eyes.

"I am going to make love to you tonight." I did.

She was a blow job. She was so thrilled, she said. "I never thought, I would ever be in this bed."

After she left, I started drinking. *This was my habit, drink little or not at all in front of other people. When everyone was gone, I drank. I learned later that was what was called a closet drinker. What had happened to my life? I used to be a nondrinker. I was very active in church. In some crazy way, I felt closer to the Lord when I was drinking. Maybe that was because I was always alone when I drank. Being alone, I had no one to communicate with, except in thought. Having lived a Christian life, naturally being free in my drunken mind to think freely about anyone or anything, Christ would come into focus.*

* * *

The next morning, I received a phone call from a lady friend that worked in a local Jewish restaurant that I frequented.

"Good morning Kirk."

"Good morning, and what gets you up so early."

"I am at work. We are having a little get together at my house tonight and I have been asked to make sure that you are there."

"And who asked you for that guarantee?"

She said, "Ivy." Just like I knew who Ivy was.

"I know a lot of people, but I can't place any one named Ivy."

"You met her last night at your house. I guess you know what it means. She told me to tell you that she was sorry that she showed no appreciation for you trying to hold her up. Does that make any sense to you?"

"I think, I know who you mean. She is tall with dark hair?"

"Yes. I have to get back to work. See you to-night."

She gave her address to me. I agreed to be there. 'Ivy.' I wonder if her eyes were telling the truth.

At the get together or party as I call it, were about 25 people. I quickly spotted Ivy.

"May I introduce myself? I am Kirk Donaldson. You were at my house last night."

"I am a little embarrassed for my behavior last night. It bothers me to have someone, that is a man touch me."

"That is what I thought. No harm done. Let us be friends. I am going to give you a chance to make up for it. Come to my house for lunch to-morrow."

"What can I bring?"

"Nothing."

Harold Morris and Joyce Axle were at my house when Ivy arrived. She brought a salad. I Bar-B-Q steak and we all enjoyed our meal except, Ivy seemed a little disappointed that I had other company. Although she and Joyce seem to get along well. They went in the house talking women talk. That gave Harold and me a chance to discuss the next few group discussions that I would be moderating.

*Moderating and public speaking have gotten me into trouble a few times because I was a persuasive talker and sometimes I spoke to the limit of my knowledge of the subject and when asked a question, I could not answer it. That has not been a problem moderating for **PWS** groups because most everyone is playing a game. The old pro is playing ignorant about sex. The new ones are pretending to know all about it.*

Harold complimented me for drawing such large groups at discussions. He said, "Clair and you satisfied most people with the discussions about sex. Anything with "sex" in the titled attracted a crowd. It was very easy to lose a group when moderating. A moderator should appear friendly. Encourage each person to speak, and discourage too much speaking from one person. A few times when inexperienced moderators lost a group, you were asked to take over, and you did and you did it well."

"Thank you Harold. We do what we can."

"Please don't mention it to anyone; but, we are going to be asked to make some sort of contribution to a CBS Sunday night special show. When I learn more about it, I will let you and Clair know."

The ladies were back. Harold and Joyce left. And Ivy invited me to come to her apartment that evening.

* * *

I wore Levies and a shirt that was unbuttoned. I leaned back on her sofa as she stood beside me. She looked at me like a hungry lion about to eat. She got on her knees and started kissing me at my stomach and continued every few inches up to my neck. While she was working her way up, I quickly unbuttoned my pants and took it out. I thought before leaving home that I should not wear shorts. When she reached my neck, she raised her head just a little and moved back where she started. She didn't seem a bit shocked or surprised to see it looking at her. Into her mouth it went for a few minutes only. Then she spoke, "You make yourself at home. I am going to take a bath."

While she was bathing, I took the liberty of going into her bedroom, where I took off my cloths and laid on her king sized bed. Turns out, a king sized bed would not really be big enough.

As she walked out of the bath room, she looked pleased to see me on her bed. She lay down and started sucking. About every minute and a half she would pull it out of her mouth and make the loudest noise I had ever heard a woman make when having an orgasm. She kept this cycle of in the mouth, a minute and a half, pull it out, climax, back in, and on, and on for I guess about twenty minutes. All over that big bed. Each time she went to put it back in her mouth, she would push or pull me into a different position. I realized the pulling out just before climaxing was to prevent biting me. This was fun. It was different. It was exciting. But; I had to shove her onto her back, and put it in between her legs so that I could climax.

She put on a robe as I got dressed. We went into her kitchen, where she gave me a piece of fruit cake and a cup of tea. She told me how she, as a child, would lay in bed at night and listen to her mother make repeated loud noises from her parent's bed room. She was now talking to me like someone she had known very well for a long time. For example she said, "I worry going with two or three different guys a week, what I may pick up."

I never heard any concern about sexually transmitted diseases. The main fear was herpes. We had not yet heard of AIDS. I personally had sex with dozens of women and never, well almost never received and transmitted anything.

I saw Ivy once or twice a week for about 3 months. I painted a room for her, and took her and her two children to Ensenada, Mexico. She always seemed a little unhappy with me. I believed it was because of our sexual mismatch. That is, she was much more highly motivated sexually than I. This was proven out by what happened in Ensenada. I got sick, very sick, with a high fever. Ivy's children slept in the car and she and I slept in my tent. No doubt Ivy had grand ideas about a wild night of sex. But I could not participate.

One final blow to our relationship came when I took her to a party where my best buddy was there with my best girlfriend, Andrea. As they say to make a long story short, my best buddy knew that I would be there with Ivy so he lined up my best girl friend to take her to the party as a joke. I did not think it was funny.

I asked Andrea to dance. Got her around the corner where we were likely not to be seen and gave her some story, that I can't remember. It worked. She accepted it. She put her arms around me and started to kiss me just as Ivy walked up. Ivy grabbed her by the shoulder spinning her around. I jumped between them.

Ivy spoke, "Kirk. Take me home before I scratch her eyes out."

I told Andrea, "Wait for me. I'll; be right back. I thought you were in New York."

I took Ivy as far as her driveway. Let her out, where she quickly walked to her car. No doubt she was going to a bar where she could pick up a guy.

* * *

At a **PWS** picnic, I spotted a woman with a baby. She must be new or I would have recognized her. She was fairly nice looking, nice figure.

Of course in the 60's and 70's there were not many fat people. The fat trend got going in the 80's.

As I introduced myself, I was being watched by many people. A friend later told me that one person said, "Watch Kirk. Next thing he will do is pick up the baby."

That was said just before I picked up the baby. I visited with her for half an hour, got her name, Shirley, address, phone number, and an invitation to lunch.

Shirley lived in a nice house in one of the better housing tracks. We had a fine roast beef meal. She told me that I was the only man to sit at that table since her divorce.

After lunch I sat in the living room while she cleaned the kitchen. The house was beautifully furnished and she was obviously a good house keeper. She came in and sat next to me on the sofa. I reached over and held a hand. She squeezed it several times, like she was trying to send a message. I kissed her, and wow she surely knew how to kiss. I didn't know whether I was still ignorant about women, or whether I did it for show. I got up. Thanked her for the lunch and walked out. She looked surprised and followed me to the car. I got in as she quickly opened the door and got in beside me. I put both arms around her, held her closely, and kissed her again, as she was un-zipping my pants. She sucked for a few minutes.

Then she said, "Come back in. I am not going to do this out here".

Back in the living room, I climaxed in her mouth. She pulled it out a little too soon and the spermato-zoa were running down her face.

I asked, "Do you ever do it the other way so I could put that stuff in your vagina?"

"Not very often" she replied.

"Do you ever have an orgasm ?"

"Once in a while, I do."

I saw Shirley three more times. Once we went to a Dodger's baseball game, and once to my home for a swim, and once I just stopped at her house.

My pool had never been so satisfying. And, I never knew a woman who could hold her breath so long. She would jump feet first into the deep end of the pool in front of me, grab my legs to stay down, then put it in her mouth and start sucking.

We dried off and went in the house. We played around in the living room.   I kissed her body all over and finally on the carpet, I got it in her vagina and she climaxed.

A few days later, she phone me to tell me she went to her doctor and learned she had a, vaginal disease that only affects women. It was commonly called yeast disease. Men pass it on to other women. I did not know if I had given it to her, or if she had given it to me. She got medicine from her doctor for herself and for me.

I stopped at Shirley's house the next day. She said that I was the only man since her x-husband. I suggested that since we both have it, we can't get it. This time we tried her bed room, vagina only.

The only one since her x-husband. Wow, what a story. Bryan Stevens had her before I did, and he had her because she was recommended by Sam Howard.

* * *

I got out of a business meeting one week day night, and driving west on the Hollywood freeway, I looked at my **PWS** bulletin. A group discussion was on my way. I seldom went to group discussions that were not moderated by Clair or myself.

The discussion was almost over when I arrive. As I walked in a Nurse who was unknown to me, fixed her eyes on me. I did a little visiting with various friends, then as I was leaving I spoke to Peggy for the first time, "Are you ready to go ?"

She answered, "Let me get my coat."

Peggy had a bachelors' degree. She was divorced, She said. However I doubted that she had ever been married. She had no children. She was an RN.

She agreed to follow my car.

Going to bed with her was like going to bed with a hungry lion. Moaning, and screaming. Nothing personal about it. She would put it in with her on top. Then pull it out and suck for a while. I think I could have put a stiff weenie in her and left the room, and she would have continued moaning and screaming. After the show was over, she told me that I was the first one since her x-husband.

More than half of the women that I had sex with said that. Many people would have difficulty believing that women have to rationalize their interest in sex.

I had a couple buddies that liked that kind of sex. I told them about her and assured them that she would be at the next party at my house.

* * *

My beautiful Andrea had told me that she and her husband use to get yeast disease occasionally. They took pills to get rid of it. And, I was the only sex partner she had had since her husband. I phoned her, and suggested she see a doctor because I believe I have yeast disease.

There was no doubt in my mind that I had gotten it from Andrea.

Doreen just got back from Hawaii where she visited with Steve (Dr Steve Parker), But worse than that she had sex with a Hawaiian lad who was getting married in a few days. I had the difficult job of phoning Ivy, Shirley, and Peggy also.

When I phoned, Ivy. She just told me a few days before that she was concerned about getting a sexually transmitted disease. Now I have to tell her that I have transmitted one to her. She knew how to avoid passing it on. Just limit the sexual activity to oral sex only.

This was the first and last sexually transmitted disease that I had heard of in the unmarried world in the 12 years that I was in it.

* * *

Lynda was my first experience with black females. I had always heard that they are highly motivated sexually. I phoned Lynda and said, "I am now going to give you the opportunity to cook in my kitchen as you said you wanted to do that night at the party."

"Thank you Kirk, I accept."

Lynda was an all around great person. She was a Christian. She was an accountant. She had a master's degree. She was a soloist. He father paid for some of the cost of busses used to transport civil rights workers to Birmingham. When she arrived at my house, she was wearing a thin t-shirt with obviously nothing on under it. She was not surprised to see that I had two other guests. A black friend of mine and his white wife.

Lynda prepared a fine Italian dinner. After eating, we sat and talked a bit. I bid (or maybe I should say "we bid) our guests good night. After cleaning the kitchen, she came into the living room where I was sitting in my big overstuffed chair. Without saying a word, she sat on my lap. We kissed a few times. Then I removed her t-shirt. Wow, what a beautiful pair of breasts.

She hadn't been asked to stay overnight but she was obviously planning to stay. I picked her up and carried her to my bed room. We both stripped and got under the covers. It was nice to cuddle with her warm, soft body. I kissed her lip, and chin, and worked my way down to her feet. She did the same to me, but no sucking. She was warm- not hot. She was loving. She was the kind of woman that I thought would make a good wife.

I was beginning to realize that one good woman, a wife, would be better than all of these sex partners that I had had. I thought about each one of them and quickly decided none of them marriageable. I realized for the first time that marriage is what I was looking for.

A few days later, she invited me to opening night at a big hotel in Beverly Hills, where I was given a front row seat in their ball room. Lynda was the star attraction. She sang beautifully. She was dressed like, wow. I sat there thinking, this beautiful woman spent the night making love to me.

She phoned me a few nights later to ask if I would check on the availability of an apartment that she had tried to rent. She had been told that it was no longer available, and she suspected she was being denied because she was black. I drove to the apartment building. When I showed my pretty white face, I was told that they had one available, that had been rented yesterday.

I will always remember her words, *"There is a difference between love and sex."* In her case I question that. She had sex with me like she was in love with me. To this day, years later, I have warm feelings for her.

* * *

Clair Norman phoned to ask if I would allow her to have a therapy group at my house.

"I wouldn't mind, Clair, except as you know, I am getting ready to go to Europe. What you don't know, I have most of my furniture in storage to protect it. I don't even have a place to sit."

"That is OK. My people will be happy to sit on the floor."

"How many of them would you expect to have?" I said while thinking, why do they want to use my house. I couldn't imagine the group being over 25.

"I will have 12, that includes you and me,"

"Why do you want a house as large as mine. Most any place could accommodate that many people."

"Kirk, I am going to just ask you to trust me. You have a pool with a view, and many other assets for this kind of group. Trust me."

The group was to start a 7:30. I was sitting on the love seat of my pool at five o'clock with a double

Scotch and soda in my hand. My German Sheppard sat beside me. She was a great lover of the pool. Even when I was not at home, she went swimming every day in warm weather. Suddenly my doorbell rang, followed by several firm knocks. I am thinking will this be one early female like at the nude group of nuts. If it is, I hope she is a bit closer to normal. I opened the door just a crack, "What can I do for you." I said to a nice looking couple standing there.

"We were asked by Clair Norman to come here for a therapy session. I am not staying, said the man, I am just transporting my girlfriend. Sorry we are so early. I have an appointment near here and agreed to bring her."

"You want to wait? I'll be right back. I have to get a robe on."

I got back and let them in. "Sorry there is no place to sit. I am moving out."

"This is a beautiful home, I'll bet you are sorry to have to leave. I want to say, I am sorry that I arrived so early. I tried phoning Clair but got no answer."

The boyfriend waved good bye and said, "If you need a ride home, phone one of the numbers that I gave you."

I said, "I'll fix you a drink if you like. I am having a Scotch and soda. Then I am getting back in the pool."

"No thanks on the drink. However I will have a glass of water"

I pointed to a glass and went back into the pool.

She walked out, looking around, taking in the view. Then she looked down at me and said, "What a beautiful view."

"Thank you, You did mean me. Right?"

"No, I Didn't. But you are nice looking too. All except one thing, where is your bathing suit?"

"I can't afford one. Did you bring one?"

She said, no. "How long until the group will be here?"

"I think about 7 or 7:30."

"Good. If you don't mind, I would like to join you in the water."

"Before you get into the water, bring that battle of whiskey with you."

She brought the whiskey with two glasses almost filled with ice. "I changed my mind; I'll have a drink with you."

"Oh, I like your bathing suit, no front, no back, no top, on bottom. Here, sit by me." I said.

She sat close, that is skin to skin. I put a hand on her upper leg.

She didn't say a word, just smiled, and she got hold of my penis.

I said, "I believe you are my kind of girl."

"Hope so."

She straddled me with folded knees.

I leaned back my head and shoulders while raising hips and penis. I slipped in. Just then Clair came round the corner of the house. Looking directly at us she said, "I am happy you two got so well acquainted."

"Do you need help Clair ", I asked.

She replied, "Let me put it this way. There are about ten more loads. I can haul them or for two people, that is five each or three times three."

I put on my robe and slippers, and said to Clair "Stay in the kitchen. I will unload the rest."

One or two at a time they came, until I counted thirteen women and no men.

Clair signaled for everyone to congregate in the den. She said, "We are all here. Time to tell Mister Donaldson the purpose for our being here. Does this date bring anything to mind Kirk? Are you ashamed to admit that you are a year older today? You have been so good about letting us use your house for parties, meetings, group discussions, and so on. That for your birthday we are going to show our appreciation by treating you to a party you will never forget." *And I never have.*

There was plenty of good looking food. I went to the food table, picked up a plate. That is as far as I got. A beautiful young lady took the plate away from me, and then asked, "What would you like to eat?"

I was fed one bite at a time. Another lovely lady helped me remove my robe.

Two of them were already nude and in the pool. Clair asked if I was ready to get in the pool. I nodded. I thought, two in the kitchen, two in the pool, and Clair moving around. Where are the other seven?

Soon after I got in the pool, the other seven showed up. One at a time, they removed their cloths and got in the pool. They formed two lines facing each other. The lines were curved. Clair gestured for me to come to the ends of the lines. I leaned back toward the lines. Soon I realized I was being floated on my back. There must have been 20 fingers on each side moving vigorously as they moved me slowly while the back of my hands rubbed each tit. The line never ended. My pool was 30 feet wide and 50 feet long. As I was moved slowly along the girls at my feet would hurry to the head of the line. This was just about the most fantastic feeling I had ever had.

After 15 minutes, I Think, Clair Suggested, "Everyone get out of the pool, get dry and come in the house."

I was the last one out. As I walked up the steps I saw I didn't need to look for a towel. Two smiling females, one on each side waited my stepping on the top step. They dried me as well as they could with me standing. I laid down on a cot. Then they dried me all over. My penis was pointing straight up. They were extra gentle drying it.

In the house a sheet was laying on the floor. Clair gestured for me to lay on it which of course I did. The girls took turns, three at a time rubbing my back and legs and feet. They used some kind of lotion. It had a nice smell. Then they asked me to turn over and they gave the same treatment to the front side. It was so relaxing that I lost my erection.

Clair announced, "That concludes you're going away party, Kirk, unless you want to choose one of these ladies to spend the night."

"They are all so lovely, it would be too hard to choose." They all left and I had a few drinks of whiskey. Was I now turning down sex for alcohol ?

I had difficulty finding anyone that would take care of my children and my dog so I canceled my trip plans and moved my furniture back into the house.

* * *

PWS people played volley ball every Monday night at a local high school gym. Some people came but did not play. They stood around and talked. Some came because they were lonely. Others came to check on the inventory of potential sex partners.

Now I am going to take a break. Let me say again that this is the true story of twelve years of my life. I write it because the truth needs to be told. Why? Because, most people believe that they are normal sexually. Many of the incidences will seem extreme to many of you. Extreme one way or the other. It is my hope that some of you will find your selves more tolerant of those with less or more sexual motivation than you.

At volley ball a sharp looking black headed woman was actively playing. Usually new people stand and wait for someone to invite them to play. She appeared to be in her late twenties, Oriental, medium height and weight, attractive. I was playing next to Bryan Stevens. He was looking at her the same as I. I said to him, "I'll flip you for her."

He shook his head and said, "No. You can have her."

I watched her until she left the playing floor.

"Good evening. My name is Kirk. What is yours?"

"Barbara."

"Barbara, I want to welcome you to **PWS.** I have just a few questions to ask if you don't mind."

"That is OK."

"I will give you an application before you leave tonight. How many children do you have?"

"Two."

"How did you hear about **PWS**?"

"A woman I work with used to belong. She met a very nice man in the club and married him."

"I suppose she told you that the primary purpose of the club is to provide for our children. It's been nice meeting you, Barbara. I hope you enjoy PWS. Oh, I forgot to tell you. The group is coming to my house tonight after play. If you would like to go, let me know."

"I'll let you know right now. Yes, I would like to go."

"I can give you directions, or you can leave when I do and ride up with me and I will bring you back later this evening."

"I'll ride with you."

"OK let's go."

About 15 to 20 came to my house. It was about 50/50 male female. This is the only **PWS** activity where the men equal the women. A good time was had by all. The group departed about eleven o'clock. Barbara was busy cleaning the kitchen. I had good feelings about her.

I walked up behind her and put my arms around her waist. She waited a couple of minutes, then turned around. I held her tightly with one leg pressing between both of hers. She was warm, very warm. I got her by the hand and we walked into the living room. I took her to the sofa and gestured for her to sit. Then I walked across the room and sat on another sofa. I felt rushed and just wanted to cool down a little. I said to her, "You are a beautiful young lady."

She responded, "Is that why you sit across the room from me?"

"You can come over here any time you like."

She slowly walked across the 20 or so feet that separated us, sat down on the floor and laid her head on my lap. I ran my fingers through her beautiful long black hair.

She spent the night. About three hours of sleep and five hours of making love. She had the most beautiful body. Her golden skin was smooth like a baby.

She had two children. I never saw them. I believe she was a good mother. Somehow I got the impression that she was enjoying her freedom and liked a variety of experiences. Bryan Stevens phoned a couple of days later asking, "Well Kirk, I saw Barbara was the last to leave Monday night. How was it?"

"Bryan, it was fantastic."

"I knew that it would be. When you asked me if I wanted to flip you for her, I was just bull shitting you when I indicated no interest. I had her about a week before. I am the one that recommend **PWS** to her. She is so hot; I thought it would be the right place for her where she could find enough guys to keep her britches cooled."

Bryan had a different experience with Barbara than I had. With me she had it in her mouth about as much as she had it in her vagina. When I cum, she quickly pulled it out of her mouth, squirted it back and forth on her cheeks, then quickly back in her mouth. With Bryan, she never had it in her mouth. Instead when it wasn't in her vagina it was in her rectum.

The next day, I got a phone call from her. She wanted to come for a visit. This life was like a buddy had in Germany during World War Two. He was Dutch, and was forced labor. During the day he labored. At night he had women by appointment only. Most of the German men were away.

Barbara came up a couple of nights later. We spent the first two hours talking. She explained how in recent years, China has been interested in reducing its population. Several decades ago the opposite was true. To insure large families, Polygamy was encouraged. Some men had several wives. One king had 121 wives, consorts, and concubines. If a woman had a lover, other than her husband, she would be punished, sometimes with death. Chinese sexual practices were passed on to

Japan. They believed females lacked something in their bodies and males had excess so they united. No original sin as in Christianity. If men cared properly for their families they could have extra-marital sex partners. Japanese women often had many husbands. They were called, " Goddesses of Mercy." They did not suffer as westerners with sex. Explicit sexual pictures were hung on the walls inside their homes. She explained that being Chinese gave her a sexual freedom that many western women do not have. Her husband was Jewish and was not in full accord with her thinking.

I told her that my experience was that American women, since the introduction of the birth control pill, have not been conservative about sex.

Bryan was wrong about the variety that she would have. She told me that Bryan had a very large male organ. And that he and I were the only men that she was dating.

* * *

Another **PWS** general meeting. I didn't see Andrea Richards. I hoped she had a compatible boyfriend.

There were many beautiful women. When the meeting was over I spotted a well dressed one, a little older than most of the ones that I had been seeing. She looked like money. I introduced myself and asked if she would like to go for something to eat. I had already been asked to go with an engineer with whom I had once worked and his steady girlfriend. He was currently one of the vice presidents of this chapter of **PWS**.

We all got along well. Gail obviously was well educated. She lived in one of the riches areas of Los Angeles. Her x-husband was a movie director. When we were let out near her car and mine, I asked if she would like to see my home. She indicated that would not be proper. I got her address and agreed to take her to a private party the next night.

When I arrived at her house the next, she got in the car and immediately there was a problem. I had one beer before leaving home. She strongly objected to picking her up with beer on my breath. I almost turned around to take her back home. Later I was glad that I did not. She was a hit at the party. She got to meet most of the officers of the club. And everyone liked her.

After the party, we got in the car and drove to an intersection where I stopped. If I turn right, I am taking her home. If I turn left, I am taking her to my house. She looked at me and said, "Why are you stopped?"

I didn't answer. I turned left. I put my arms around her and we had a big kiss. I let one arm on her shoulders. She got hold of my hand pulled it under her arm and put it on her breast. She said, "I am very soft." I learned that "soft"met sagging. When arriving at my house, I looked at her and said, the dumbest question of the day, "Would you like to come in?"

I took her out in the back yard to let her view the lights in the valley below.

Then directly to the bed room. I started removing her cloths and then my own. She had a beautiful white body that I loved to kiss. She licked and kissed most of me.

She said, "That was the first, oral sex I ever had."

I believed her. It lasted almost an hour.

Then she said, "She tried to go down on her husband once and it through him into counseling. That son of a bitch. He always told me about how wonderful his mother was. If he admired his mother so much why didn't the son of a bitch marry her?"

I wondered, is she like many of the Jewish women that I had met, that pushed their husbands constantly to make more money. Some of these men worked so hard that they were not in shape for sex when they got home from work. This was the first woman that I believed when she said I was the first one since her x-husband. She came from a rich New York Jewish family. Her husband was the first one she had sex with and that was on their honey moon.

She asked, "What is your religion?"

"Could you not guess by now. I am Jewish of course."

A week later she told me she had written to her mother that, she had finally met a Jewish man with no hang ups.

We had a campout coming up. I asked Gail to go. She said yes and that she wanted to take her children. We all spent the night before the camp out at my house. Her children used two of the guest rooms. I started a little necking in the living room. She was quick to say, "No. Not with the children in the house."

The campout was great. About a hundred people in attendance. About half had never been camping, including Gail and her children. I set up my big tent with four sleeping bags in it. We joined a sing-a-long group around a fire. I soloed one song. Few knew that I could sing. My nick name among some of them was Nelson Eddy. A couple of others soloed quite well.

I think part of that group kept singing until well after midnight. Gail tucked in her little ones. Then she and I went for a walk, holding hands. Soon, I announced, "I am getting tired. Let's sit in the car for a while."

Of course once in the car, we could not keep our hands off each other. She split the time, half oral and half conventional.

The following week, she went with me to a group discussion that I was moderating. It was the first time she had seen me leading a group. As we left, she said, "You should be president of something, and I don't mean **PWS**."

Statements like that were typical from females that thought they had one guy hooked. They started making unkind remarks about **PWS***, trying to persuade their lover to stay away from the club. You can guess the real reason, competition.*

Back at her house, we went into the maid's quarters (She did not have a maid. She had a once a week cleaning lady). The only undressing was my pants and shorts. She started licking and sucking. Then in her sweet New York Jewish voice said," I am beginning to really like this."

I never ejaculated in her mouth. It took a lot of practice to be able to avoid it during all of that sucking. But; I waited until the panties came off and put it where it belonged.

One night her husband had the children so she invited me to stay overnight. She went to bed while I was going over some paperwork at her dining room table. She had been curious as to how I could live in a million dollar house and drive a new Cadillac when I never seem to work. The answer was simple, she just happened to meet me during one of my periods of unemployment. She walked by the table and saw an official looking paper from the United States government. Actually it had to do with my past port.

However the next morning as we were eating breakfast she looked up at me with a serious look on her face,

"You work for the government. Don't you."

Before I answered, I thought about it, this lady is obviously intelligent; But, Also very naive. Actually, most of my work was government.. However working as a physicist is not the kind of work she had in mind.

"I am not allowed to talk about it."

"Is your work dangerous?"

"I don't concern myself with that. Somebody has to do it."

One night I sprained my ankle playing volley ball. I went to Gail's house and when she asked why I was limping. I didn't give a straight answer. I hinted that it had happened when I parachuted into a foreign country.

She asked, "You poor darling. Is there anything that I can do to help?"

"Just give me lots of loving."

One thing it would kill Gail to know. A couple of times she let her twelve year old daughter alone with me. The first time, I was watching television and she walked across the room between me and the television set to make sure that I noticed her. When she got to me, without asking she sat on my lap. I just made sure my hands were stretched out far from her. The second time, I was sitting up reading. She sat on the floor next to me, raised up a little and put her bent elbow right on my penis. I got up and changed books

* * *

It was the first night at Monday night volley ball for Lois. A sharp looker, about 25 year's old, Jewish, nice figure, two children, lived in North Hollywood, and no doubt her x-husband was a son-of-a-bitch. The only thing different about this one from the majority was she owned her own home, i.e., she didn't rent an apartment.

I struck up a conversation and had her follow me to a local café after the games. I told her that I was planning a trip to Europe. We just had normal small talk. When we left, I suggested that I follow her home. She said, "You are going to Europe. I want someone here."

"I will be here for a while."

I followed her home. She had a large living room, But we sat in a small den with only a couch. She asked, "Do you want anything to eat."

"Just, well nothing. I'll take a drink if you have one".

She laughed and said, "Come with me for something better than a drink".

Now this was a new kind of record, I did not kiss her; I did not hold hands with her.

This night, I will never forget. Rather conventional, copulate with her lying on her back, me lying on top of her. It was like we had been married for several years.

The following Monday night she was at the volley ball again. I said hello, and asked if she wanted a little after the game activity. She nodded her head. As we were walking out of the gym I asked if she wanted to stop for refreshments. She didn't.

She was a very decisive person, like when she took me by the hand and walked me to her bed room the previous week. As we walked into her house she said that I should make myself at home, help myself to the liquor, and she quickly vanished. I sat on the same little couch. In a few minutes, she showed up wearing a very shear night gown. "I am not going to ask you what you want to eat because I remember your answer last week. So would you like a sandwich?"

"Sounds good."

I ate my sandwich while she was feeling my penis through my pants. I stood up in front of her while she unzipped my pants, took it out and put it in her mouth. This was a change from the first time we were together. *This was common. Most women just lie on their backs the first time, and then go wild each time thereafter. Why, I asked myself. It happens almost every time. They are trying to prove something. I don't know what.*

The following Monday night she was at volley ball again. She was becoming my steady Monday night date. I wondered what surprise she had for tonight. I found out soon after arriving at her house. She asked, "Have you ever smoked Marijuana."

"No."

"What it does, it increases whatever mood you are in . I have noticed you don't get excited about sex. Don't get me wrong. You are good. Very good. But you should get more excited."

We took off all of our cloths and got into her bath tub. She had a lighted marijuana cigarette. We took turns puffing on it. It was very strong. All it did for me was making me sleepy and hurt my throat. We went to bed and I fell asleep.

She explained later that she smokes less than a pack of cigarettes a month, and marijuana is only for special occasions.

* * *

Gail and three other women got together at a bar and restaurant along Ventura Boulevard one day for lunch and conversation. One mentioned that she had met the nicest guy at **PWS**. He moderates a lot of group discussions. One said that sounds like Kirk. The other confirmed that was the name of her new boyfriend. Another spoke up and said she did not know how she could claim him as a boyfriend when he has been going home with her girlfriend every Monday night after volley ball. And he spends the night. Another one said Kirk probably holds the world's record in having the largest number of females in any time period.

Gail phoned the next day crying, "Kirk how could you do it to me? You are a liar. What do you really do for a living? And don't give me that bull shit about being Jewish."

"I am sorry. You are a sweet wonderful lady who is very naive. When you guessed that I worked for the government, I should have explained that I am self employed in physics. I work contract, mostly government contracts. I never claimed to be Jewish. My mother is Jewish. That makes me Jewish according to some Jewish authorities. As far as our relationship goes, it was great, but I never told you that you were my one and only. I was raised a Christian. I practice Christianity. I attend church regularly. No Gail. I never lied to you. But I am sorry that I allowed you to believe your own assumptions."

I saw her one more time. I just happened to be near her neighborhood and so I stopped. She had company. A mutual female friend with a gentleman, no doubt to introduce to Gail as a replacement for what she thought she had in me. When they started to leave, I started also. Gale looked up at me and said, "You don't have to leave."

I walked with the two guests to the door, closed it and came back. She was still sitting on the sofa. I stood in front of her. She kissed the right spot on my Levies and then quickly looked up. That was the last time I saw her.

Was this kiss to remind me of what she used to do to me that she will not be doing anymore? No. I believe she was telling me that she still wanted to have sex with me even though we were not friends'

* * *

Another Monday night at the high school gym. As the evening went on Barbara was playing volley ball. Lois came in and started to play. Erna joined in, and finally Andrea show up. All of this kept me busy. I had informal relationships with each one of them and didn't want to hurt any ones feelings. I realized that Andrea would expect me to at least go with her somewhere after the games to have a serious talk. Erna would want something similar. Lois would likely expect me to go home with her, Barbara, I don't know. She is free lanced as am I. What to do?

I had an answer. At the end of the games, I asked everyone to come to my house. The ladies all understood that with a house full, I can't give individual attention.

Toward the end of the evening, I suggested to Barbara that she announce her leaving, go out the front door, through the gate, duck going by the rear windows and come into my bedroom via the rear door. To each of the others, I said I was tired (which I was) and will be retiring soon after everyone left (which I did).

Barbara was waiting on the bed. I got my expected blow job. At the end, she pulled it out of her mouth for a second or two, just long enough to shoot it on her cheeks, and then quickly back into her mouth, knowing that was when I had the most feeling.

* * *

One of those rare times that I attended a group discussion that Clair or I was not moderating. It was at the apartment of Betty Clayton a newly widowed woman. She was in her early thirties, had a very nice figure. She was Jewish, and had two pre-teen aged children. She seemed in a hurry to meet mister right and get married. She didn't know anything about me. She made the mistake of believing that I was a good potential mate.

She had prepared some very nice deserts. She looked at me and said, "You can have all you want of anything", as I looked at the fine spread. I got to chat with her some. I invited her to my house for the next night.

She showed up in time for dinner. I had prepared a rotisserie chicken. (This was a misleading thing. I bought a rotisserie chicken.) She said it was the first time a man ever cooked a meal for her. She was a little surprised when I said grace before starting to eat. After we finished our meal, we sat in the living room and talked about our histories. She had a laceration on her arm with liquid bandage covering it. I said, "Too bad. Otherwise we could go swimming."

She said, "I can swim."

She obviously did not have a bathing suit. So she went in one of the bed rooms, and removed all of her clothing, put on a robe, and returned to the hall where I was waiting, also wearing a robe. I went out to the pool, and with my back facing her, dropped my robe and jumped in the water. She quickly disrobed where she was standing, walked out to the pool and carefully walked down the pool steps. As she slowly walked toward me, I dove under the water and swam to her. I rose up against her, arms around her, holding her tightly. We played a little in the water. She liked to hold onto my penis. I had two big beach towels waiting. We got out of the pool, we went over to two chaise lounges and lay down. We held hands while we talked.

The air got a little chilly so we went into the living room with our towels and laid on them on the floor. I looked over at all of that beauty, back and forth. I started kissing it on the feet and gradually worked my way up to the head.

"Can you stay all night?"

"Yes, if you think we can find enough things to do to keep busy."

"I think we can. Shall we try the bed room?"

"OK."

"Would you like a drink before going to bed?"

"What do you have?"

"Beer, wine, Bourbon, Scotch"

"I will have a glass of wine."

I thought, *she is Jewish. Most Jews don't drink heavy.*

In bed, I was in no hurry. I just loved her body pressing against mine. I thought, I would like this every night. Oral sex? I tried. She didn't.

We were at it so much that I asked, "You have been without for a while?"

"Kirk, I have been without for close to four years. It sure feels great to be back with it again."

I did not hurry. I believed at one time, I had it in her for an hour. Just wiggle a little occasionally, kiss, hug. Our bodies became very wet. We enjoyed it. We could slide around on each other.

The thought occurred to me, *"This would make a wonderful wife. But, Would I miss the oral sex that I had come to enjoy? Can this gal cook? I'll bet she can. Those homemade goodies at her apartment were good. I forgot, she has children. I wondered, do I want more children. Mine are on their own much of the time. Do I want a wife? I would trade a lot of freedom for locking in on my one and only. I will keep looking for a wife. What would I do if I found the perfect wife and she objected to my drinking.*

I guess, I would just stop drinking. I thought it would be easy."

I saw her two more times, once at a group discussion that I was moderating and once at a party at my house. I really felt sorry for her. All she wanted was a husband; but with two children she has little chance.

* * *

Visiting at a friend's house, two ladies in their mid-twenties were just leaving as I arrived. They both seemed less interested in leaving after I met them. They each had warm eyes. We talked for a few minutes. I got Rebecca's phone number.

I phoned her the next day. And we arranged to go to the snow up in the mountains that day, taking her two children with us. Her son was five years old and her daughter was two years old. We all enjoyed the day, making a snow man and throwing snow balls.

Back at her house that evening, she prepared a simple dinner.

Jewish women are without a doubt better at preparing meals then are non-Jews. I have been to genital's homes where I was given a sandwich that consisted of two slices of bread with a little something in between. A Jewish woman prepares a sandwich that one has to open wide to get a bite.

She bathed the children and put them to bed. I was sitting on the couch looking at a newspaper when she came in and asked me if I wanted a glass of wine. I drank the first one quickly and had a second and third. I told her I had a big day coming up and had to get to bed early. She looked surprised and a little disappointed. We made a date for a few nights later.

Two nights later, I stopped at her house after dinner. She was pleased to see me.

"Come in Kirk. This is a pleasant surprise. I thought you would phone first. Don't get me wrong, I am so happy to see you. Have a seat. I am just putting the children to bed. I'll be with you in a moment."

She had a small house. About 900 square feet, I would guess. Three very small bedrooms. No television in the living room. That pleased me and told me something about her. I had one TV. It was built in the ceiling above my bed).

"Well Kirk, would you like a glass of wine?"

"Yes. That sounds good."

I should have realized as I sat on her couch with this lovely, warm, 28 year old pushing up against me;

I was more interested in consuming glass after glass of wine. That should have indicated an illness. I never seemed to get drunk. I heard a statement years later, "One is too much, and many are not enough." I was realizing what that meant.

We started doing some hot necking, and soon ended up in her den on a little half sized bed. She on her back and me on top of her. To a guy that has been married for years, that would seem exciting; but, to me after what I had been going through since my wife left, it was downright dull. However I could guess, the next time would be different.

That was a Thursday night. As I left, I told her, "I will be back Saturday. I am not much on dating, so if you can think of anything you would like to do together, just let me know."

CHAPTER 11

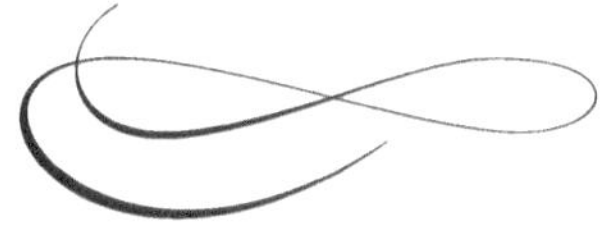

One Sunday morning, I decided to skip going to my church in favor of going to the largest Lutheran church in the San Fernando Valley. During the service I looked at the row behind me and saw a nice looking pair of legs partially under a short skirt. After service I went in the social hall for coffee. There she was, standing with a little girl about three years old holding her hand. I went to work. Within five minutes I had her phone number, address, and arrangement to visit her that evening.

She was not and had never been married. Her daughter fell in love with me almost immediately. We talked and I played with her daughter until bed time for the little one. After tucking her in she came back in the living room and sat down beside me. I used my many months of experience, tried every approach I could think of and all I got was "no".

She had quite a story to tell. Her father owns a manufacturing business in Illinois in a small town. When she got pregnant by a service man who was in Germany when her family learned of her pregnancy. To avoid embarrassment her father agreed to help her move to some other part of the country. She has been here for a few years, communicates regularly with her lover in Germany and will not get sexually involved with anyone else.

As I was driving home, I thought to my self, "*You can't win them all.*"

I looked at the church bulletin and found a Tuesday night Bible study for singles and unmarried's.

Tuesday night I went to a private home for the study. About fifteen to twenty people in attendance. After the study they had a social hour with cookies and coffee. Two people were talking about the pros and cons about dating. Soon the entire group was involved. I was surprised when the hosts daughter told the group that she completely stopped dating because she was apposed to sex outside of marriage and just getting close to a man caused her to come home in a sweat.

Another female in the group seemed quiet. She sat by herself a little out of the group. I went to her, said hello and introduced myself. She was a slow talker. Something about her, I did not know what, made her not appealing. However she said that she had walked to the Bible study and if I didn't mind I could give her a ride home.

She lived in a very small house in the back yard of another house. I just stopped and said, "It was a pleasure meeting you. I hope to see you again sometime."

"You could walk me to the door, if you don't mind."

"No problem. I would be happy to do that."

At the door, she invited me in. I had nothing better to do. She was a much bigger talker at home than she had been at the Bible study. She told me that she was a Roman Catholic Nun. She got pregnant and so had to leave the church. That was six years before. She joined the Lutheran church with her son who was then five years old. She had never been married.

Run away Catholics usually end up in Lutheran churches.

I saw her in church the following Sunday. She invited me to lunch at her house after church. I accepted. This time I got to meet her son. He was not pleasant to be around. I didn't stay long. She wanted to talk more. I gave her my phone number and left.

Soon after arriving home, she called. She pleaded with me to come back that evening. I couldn't understand what the problem was but it must be important so I agreed to come.

She met me at her gate, about 15 feet before her front door.

"I am so glad you could make it. Come in. Sit on the couch."

"Well, I am here. So what is so important"

" It is very important to me. I am considering changing churches. I want your opinion."

"I am afraid my opinion is not worth much on that subject."

"Oh OK. I just thought I would try. Do you mind if I sit there with you?"

"It's your house."

She sat down the side of me with her legs across my lap. I quickly put one hand across the back of the couch and held the other up.

She said, "You don't have to hold your hand up unsupported like that. You can put it on my leg."

She reached over and pushed my hand down onto the closest leg to my chest. That put my fingers between her legs. I moved my hand just a little up her leg. She smiled. I moved it further. She kept smiling. I moved it all the way. She was wearing no Panties. I went ahead and had sexual relations with her.

I had gotten used to women telling me that I was the first since their ex-husband. This gal took the cake. She told me that she had had sex one time in her life and got pregnant. That was over five years ago. She never had sex again until that night.

As I drove home, I told myself, this is an evening I would like to forget about. I am sorry that I gave her my phone number.

Two days later, I was out on business. When I returned home, I parked in the driveway to go in the front door. I started to unlock the door when I realized it was already unlocked. Suddenly the door swung open. There was Pattie standing there with her arms held out. The foyer was generously decorated with flowers. "What in the hell in going on here."

"I know Kirk that you don't want to get married right now. But whenever you are ready I will be here. Dinner is almost ready."

"How did you get in here?"

"I have a friend who is a lock smith. He opened the door for me."

I couldn't eat. I was very upset. I went in the master bed room and lay down on the bed. Very soon she came in to find out if I was OK.

I was going to start the process right then to get rid of her. I told her to sit in a chair. I took out my penis rubbed it on her face. She grabbed it and put it in her mouth. She worked like a pro. When I was almost ready to ejaculate, I pulled it out of her mouth. And she asked me to put it back and don't stop.

That didn't work so I told her, "I am moving out and I will move back in right after you vacate my house."

She had some serious problems. She smoked about two packs a day, and between her legs she smelled like dead fish, even with my nose four feet away.

I was gone only three days. She vacated. I returned.

CHAPTER 12

Friday night, I went to a Singles Group at a large Baptist church in the Van Nuys area. They were for the most part much younger than I. One very nice looking young lady that appeared to be about 21, approached me,

"Welcome to our group. Are you Baptist?"

"No. I claim no particular denomination. I am just a Christian."

"Would you like some punch?"

"Sounds good to me."

"I am the elected leader of the group. Let me introduce you around."

I thought to myself, this girl is not just very nice look-ing, she is beautiful. About 5 feet 4 inches tall, 110 pounds, 32B, very light completion, blond.

She handed a glass of punch to me. Then introduced me to several young people and to the Associate Pastor. The Pastor and I seem to have things of mutual interest to talk about so we retired to his office where we could sit comfortably. He had spent a few years in India. He liked to talk, and he gave me a real education on India. We discussed the philosophy that in India, Religion and sexuality were insepa-rable. Or put another way, spirituality and sexuality were inseparable. Artists and writers used sex to show their love for God. These are true in various religions (or denominations we might call them), namely Hin-du, Forth, Taoist, Shinto, and Sikh. The Kama Sutra sex manual popular at that time points out 30 sex-ual positions, four kinds of love, and eight stages of oral intercourse. It suggests solutions to each sexual problem and gives information on courtship and marriage. The frankness of this guy startled me.

"I welcome you to our church. I certainly hope you will attend, and if you get interested enough, we will make you a teacher of the Bible. I will ask Angela to work on you."

We went back to the main hall. Angela saw us immediately. She came to us and said,

"Pastor, shame on you. You took Kirk away from the party."

I quickly said, "The Pastor and I found a lot to talk about."

The Pastor said, "Angela, we have to work on this guy. He would make a great addition to our congregation."

I said, "Angela, I have a suggestion. As soon as you feel comfortable in leaving, let's go to a restaurant where we can sit and talk, without interruptions and with a little less noise."

"I am ready now."

I held the car door open for her.

"Thank you. This is the first time I ever left alone with a man."

"Well, let us pray that it is something you will cherish and never regret. We can go anywhere you like."

"The Holy Land!"

"OK. I'll have to stop at my house and get some cloths, and"

"Wait a minute. I really think you are serious."

"I am. I said anywhere you like and you said the Holy Land."

"By the way, where are we going?" She looked worried. After considerable time, she said, "I have never been alone with a man at night. Can I trust you?"

"What do you think? Can you trust me? If you think you can't, I'll take you back to church, or to your home, or where ever you want to go."
I was very surprised, "Tell me about yourself."

"What do you want to know", she asked?

"I want to know all about you; age, status, your relationship to the Lord."

"I am 23, never been married; I gave my life to Jesus when I was 15. Now tell me about yourself,"

"23. If you lived in India, your parents would have chosen a husband for you eleven years ago. I am 39 years old. Divorced with two children. I have a PhD in Physics, I work contract, that is off and on. I have spent much of my time working for the church. I have taught a few Bible classes. I am past chairman of the board of Christian Stewardship, and past Chairman of the Board of Trustees. And we are almost to my house."

"Wow! This beautiful place is yours?"

"This is the Lord's house. The Lord has blessed me by allowing me to live here. Come in. Make yourself at home. Would you like a tour of the place."

"That would be nice."

"The children live with me. However my daughter is away at boarding school and my son is, I hate to say it, is in custody of the Los Angeles County Juvenile Authority."

'I am very sorry to learn about your son. I suppose you would prefer to not talk about it."

"No I don't mind talking about it. He is a fine young man. It is a nice warm night. Would you prefer to sit outside? The view is beautiful from up here on the hill."

"Outside sounds good to me."

"What can I get you to drink? Anything, hot or cold."

"Now you are going to get to know me a little better. I don't drink coffee, or soda with caffeine. So juice, any kind will do nicely."

I brought two glasses of orange juice and handed one to her as she was leaning back on the lounge. I thought she may notice my staring at her. She was beautiful.

This is a new experience for me. Usually by now she would be on the bed. What would I think about spending the rest of my life with this beautiful woman? Is she frigid? Has she been fighting the urge for years? Maybe she is normal, average. I am not sure what that is; But, I am sure she would claim it as a description of her. After the wild women that I have been with, could I settle down with someone like this?

"I am sorry. I got to day dreaming after looking at how beautiful you are. My son. I told you I would tell you about him. While visiting with his grand parents he took a gun belonging to a neighbor, brought it home, and took it to the park where he was playing with some of his friends. He showed the gun to his buddies. They each handled it. One boy aimed it at another, pulled the trigger, not knowing it was loaded, and seriously injured the other boy. My son, not knowing what to do, hid the gun, and told the police that some passerby had shot his friend. The other boys supported his report. During interrogation at police headquarters each boy gave a different description of the alleged assailant. So they are all being held until the police get a true accounting. The victim is doing well. I expect it will all be cleared up by tomorrow."

"I don't know what to say, except I will pray for you and your son."

"Thank you. I would appreciate that. Enough of that kind of talk. What do you like? Other than church, that is."

"I like nature, fishing, and reading."

"How much education do you have? If you don't mine my asking."

"I have a bachelors' degree in psychology."

"Oh no. My wife had the same."

"Sorry. What happened to your marriage?"

"I thought we were going to have no more sad stories. I will answer you. My wife was very popular in college. She got her BS a year ahead of me. I kept going to school for a total of eight and a half years and worked part time. She got lonesome being left alone so much. She started seeing other men. Got involved. Left. I divorced her. It was uncontested. I got custody of the children, two of our three houses, and almost everything else. That is just about it. Now it is my turn to ask a question. How many boyfriends do you have." as I smiled.

"I have ten or twelve. I kind of lost count. No. I am only kidding. I had a few not very serious boy friends in high school and college. Since then, I don't know. Men my age usually don't seem mature. I have an occasional date. Nothing serious."

"What would you do if I got up, leaned over and kissed you?"

"I think that would be very nice."

And it was very nice. She had soft, damp lips.

I could have picked her up and carried her to the master bed, and spent the next ten years holding her in my arms.

"I guess I should take you back to your car at the church."

I stopped at her car in the church parking lot, jumped out quickly, went around and opened the door for her. She got out, stood in front of me looking up like she wanted me to do something. I put both arms around her and held her tightly.

She said, "I feel like I would like to go back to your house."

"I think I had better leave while I still can, and drive back home."

"Why? Do you have to get up early? It is only a little after ten."

"No, I don't have to get up early, and I would like to spend the rest of my life talking to you."

"Kirk, our group is having a picnic next Saturday. I would be very happy if you could come."

She gave the address to me and I showed up for the picnic. We sat at a table. She held my hand like we were long time lovers. Several of her friends seem to notice. After we ate, she got up and introduced me to the group. Little by little, her friends stopped and talked to me. I thought that I had been accepted by the group. At the conclusion of the picnic I carried everything to my car. I asked, "Are you ready."

Back at her apartment, she invited me in and directed me to the sofa, and said, "I will be back in a few minutes."

She came back in a few minutes, dressed as she had been before.

That made me happy because she was so beautiful that if she had returned with something sexy, it would have motivated me in a way that I don't want to be motivated.

She walked directly to me and sat on my lap saying, "I hope you don't mind."

"Angela, I need to tell you something. I am very highly motivated sexually, and you are a beautiful woman. There for, it is not a good idea for you to sit on my lap. I think maybe I should leave. Please don't get me wrong, I have very warm, loving feelings toward you. I respect you."

"When we were together at your house. You asked if you could kiss me, and I said yes. Now it is my turn, may I kiss you ?"

"Of course."

"You are looking for trouble, kissing like that. I think I had better leave."

I left, went home and phoned her to give thanks for the picnic and the kiss. We were on the phone for almost an hour. We made a date for the following Saturday night.

I picked her up, took her to dinner, and then asked if she would like to spend the rest of the evening at my house.

"Can I trust you?"

"No."

She sat on a sofa. I sat across the room.

"Kirk, I am going to tell you frankly, I am a virgin. Hard to believe? I am going to leave here tonight, still a virgin. It is not easy for me. You are a very attractive man. I would just love to go to bed with you and have you hold me in your arms. But since I have waited for twenty three years, I can wait until the ring is on the finger and our Lord has blessed my marriage."

"I have a response to that statement. I respect your right to do just what you plan to do. However, I am going to come over to your side of the room, sit down on the couch beside you, put my arms around you, kiss you, and hold you tightly. Then....?"

This was a warm woman. As I kissed her, I could feel the heat in her lips and in her mouth. As I hugged her, I felt the warmth of her body. I kissed her again, and this time I felt a hot tongue. I reached down and lightly touched one of her breasts then looked into her eyes. They seem to say OK. I removed my arms from around her, got on the floor in front of her, raised my head and kissed both of her breasts thru her blouse.

"Go to bed with me. I think I can control myself. Anything you say goes."

I got up, stood in front of her, reach down and grasped both of her hands, pulling just a little. She stood. I hugged and kissed her again. Then I picked her up, one arm under her legs, the other around her back, and carried her to the king bed.

I said, "I am going to leave you for a few minutes. When I get back, I hope you will be under the covers."

I went for a short walk just to give her privacy.

When I returned she was laying on her back looking at the ceiling. The room was dimly lighted. I stepped back a few yards, removed all of my cloths and got in under the covers with her. She turned and faced me. I put one arm under her and the other on top of her upper arm. We kissed. Her lips were as hot as before. I gently pushed her onto her back, crawled head first down to her feet. I started kissing and licking, first her feet, then her legs. I skipped where her legs joined. I kissed her stomach, chest and neck. Then very gently licked her breasts and sucked her nipples. Then I moved quickly to where my face was touching her pubic hair. I spread her legs and put my tongue into action. After about five minutes she made the loudest howl. I eased up the tongue action for about a minute, and then gradually went back to it until another howl. I moved until we were face to face. A little kiss on her forehead. There was just enough light that I could see a pretty smile on her lips. She was still a virgin. We both went to sleep.

We seemed to awaken at the same time. She rolled over into my arms, looked at me and gave that angelic little smile.

I spoke, "You are still a virgin."

"I am in love with you Kirk."

"Needless to say, I have very loving feelings for you."

"Are you hungry? If you don't mind me using your kitchen, I will cook breakfast for you."

"You are too beautiful to also cook."

I watched her nude for the first time as she got out of bed. I thought this is the most beautiful sight,

I have ever seen. She put on her panties, picked up the bra walked over to my side of the bed, and asked, "Will you hook it for me?"

After I hooked it, she looked down at me, and gave me a kiss on each cheek.

As I was driving her back to her church, she told me that her church has a group going to Israel in two months. It cost $1,800 per person. She had $400 and believed that the other $1400 would come from somewhere.

I told her that I certainly hoped she would get it. I didn't know whether she was asking me for the money or not. If she was, I would be very disappointed.

* * *

Saturday afternoon I stopped at Rebecca's house. After ringing the door bell and knocking a few times, I walked the street that went beside her house, and found her with a shovel digging in the dirt.

"What are you doing Rebecca?"

"Oh. Hi Kirk. I am trying to fill in this hole. Go back around to the front door. I'll meet you there."

"Let me guess. You were putting the last few shovels full on the grave of your estranged husband. Right?"

"No. How are you Kirk?"

"I am fine. Where are the little ones?"

"Mat picked them up this morning. He will have them until mid-day tomorrow. That gives us lots of time to play. I am going to get in the tub. Would you care to join me?"

"No thanks. I showered a short while ago. Leave the bath room door open. If you need someone to wash your pussy just yell."

"Very funny. Just make yourself at home."

I looked the house over for the first time. She was a very neat, clean housekeeper. I went in the bath and noted how nice she looked in the nude. This was the first time I had seen her nude. It was rather dark two nights ago.

"Have you decided where you would like to go or what you want to do tonight?"

"Yes, if you don't mind, it has been a long time since I have been to a restaurant."

"Say no more. I will take you to White Horse for a fine dinner."

I started my dinner with two double Scotch and sodas. She had a glass of wine. That seemed to be about right for a Jew. They just don't hit the booze. We had a fine dinner. She was so appreciative. She said, "That was the finest meal that I have had in a long time. I will have to find a way to adequately show my appreciation when we get back to the house."

When we got to her house, she excused herself and said, "Make yourself comfortable, I'll be right back."

When she returned, I was sitting on her couch. She walked over to the dining area, picked up a chair and carried it back to the middle of the living room where she sat down. She looked at me sitting about six feet away, held up one hand and motioned with her index finger to come to her. I didn't know what she had in mind so I just sat there and thought about it. Finally she said, "Come here Kirk, I want to show my appreciation for dinner."

I got up, walked to her, stood directly in front of her. She reached out and unzipped my pants. I immediately got an erection that made it too difficult for her to get my penis out of my shorts. So I dropped my pants and my shorts. She was obviously very experienced. I ejaculated in her mouth. She immediately pushed me away and said, "I always run quickly to the bath room and spit it out."

I don't think she realized that saying that made it very impersonal.

I visited Rebecca once or twice a week for almost a year. Each visit was a little different.

Once she told me how much she appreciated my visits because it eliminated the necessity of her going to Jack's office. Jack's office was a bar that was a popular pick up place. "I knew when I went; it was only for one reason."

No doubt she had conventional sex with each pick up from Jack's office, just as she did with me the first time.

Once she told me she was pregnant. The one that made her that way was a new member of **PWS** that she had over one evening. When she told him she was pregnant he gave her fifty dollars and disappeared. She wanted to borrow four hundred dollars from me for an abortion.

At another visit she told me that she had enrolled in a class for Jews that want to become Christians. She believed that we were well matched sexually, and for that reason marriage was possible. I guess she was right, we were well matched sexually.

At each visit, I received a blow job. I would sit or lay in the living room, each time in a different position. After she put the children to bed she would catch me in any position and do her thing. Of course, I always had it out and ready.

After a year I decided I wanted to break it off with Rebecca. I thought I knew how. As I was standing in front of her as she sat on the sofa, just as I started to ejaculate in her mouth, I pulled out and shot that stuff all over her face. It didn't work. She smiled. She liked it.

I did not understand how she and so many others got sexual satisfaction just sucking on a penis, nothing touching their vagina, and no climax. I had a few of them say how great I was sexually, when I had contributed nothing. Shooting that stuff all over her face, I guess would have added to my greatness.

CHAPTER 13

I visited Clair Norma in the hospital after she had had some surgery. She decided to give me some good advice, "Kirk you are having some female Problems.

What you want is some one to clean your house, cook your meals, and not interferer with your social life. Right? Here is what I suggest you do; put an ad in the local paper. Ad to read like this, 'BACHELOR SEEKS LIVE IN COOK AND HOUSE KEEPER. ROOM AND BORD IN EXCHANGE FOR COOKING AND CLEANING.' I assure you Kirk, there are hundreds of women out there that will accept this kind of offer."

I went to the news paper the next morning. The ad writer suggested a change. The ad appeared in the paper two days later. It read, 'BACHELOR SEEKS LIVE IN COOK AND HOUSE KEEPER. ROOM AND BOARD IN EXCHANGE FOR DUTIES.'

I wondered what interpretation readers would give to "DUTIES". I received 42 calls the first day. But I violated my idea of 'cook, clean and leave me alone'. I started evaluating the callers based on friendliness, and how sexy I guessed they would be.

I interviewed about 15. Finally I accepted a tall (about 5'9"), well-built that had been working as a nude dancer. She was an outstanding cook. Could clean the house quickly and efficiently.

The only TV was built in above my bed. The second night that she was there, I told her that I was going to bed and would be watching the news on the TV. She said, "Do you mind if I join you?"

"No. Not at all. It will be on in fifteen minutes. That will give me time to brush my teeth and get into my pajamas."

I got in bed nude. She walked in wearing a short gown and as best I could tell that was all she was wearing. Needless to say I missed the news. This gal was a pro. If she had not worked as a prostitute

I would be surprised. Constant moaning and groaning. I felt like I could have stuck a weenie in her and left the room, she would not notice.

She lasted three months. A good friend of mine phoned to talk to me when I was not at home. Candy took the call. They had never met. They talked for over an hour. Joe phoned again after I got home. He announced that Candy would like to move in with him if I didn't get angry. I said, "Joe under one condition, as long as you and I continue to be good friends."

Joe was up the next morning and moved her out.

* * *

About two or three nights a week I was home alone. Those nights I ate very little because I found that I got a quicker effect from alcohol. Mostly I just drank scotch, bourbon, and wine. I didn't care which. About half of the time I would get so drunk that I feared that I was about to die. I would get on my knees in front of the toilet, stick my finger down my throat until up came my dinner.

Before starting my evening of getting drunk, I phoned Angela as I had every week since that night. She invited me to go to church with her the next day. I just couldn't say, "No". I just melted when I heard her voice.

When I saw her as she opened the door my heart started beating harder. We had a few minutes so she invited me in. We hugged each other. It was difficult to let go and leave.

On the way to church, she told me that she was not included in the group that was going to Israel.

I told her, "That is too bad. I have never been there myself. I have studied about the place. I hope someday I'll be able to go."

She said, "Maybe we….."

She didn't finish her sentence.

The church service was great. I knew all of the songs except one. Great sermon. The subject was Sin.

"Sin can be said to be cheating, ridiculing, betraying, or abandoning someone. Think about the effect on your family, your church, and your acquaintances when you are guilty of sin. Think about the accumulation of sin since Adam was tempted with the apple. This was what Christ had to bear at the time of his death and resurrection."

The pastor remembered me. He was very friendly and asked me to come back any time

I held the door for Angela to get in the car. I looked at her and asked, where would you like to go for lunch?"

She said, "To my apartment. I am going to prepare lunch for you."

"I don't expect a very good meal because any one as beautiful as you couldn't also be good at cooking lunch."

It was a delicious meal. After she cleared the dishes, she served pineapple upside down cake and tea. Then she looked at me like she had something serious on her mind.

"Kirk, I don't understand. I don't understand you. It seems like you are as attracted to me as I am to you. Frankly it has been difficult for me to go so long without seeing you. That night at your house, I will never forget. The whole evening was wonderful."

"Angela, my love. You beautiful and wonderful lady. I think about you every day. When I say my prayers before going to bed, I ask God for guidance in dealing with you. When I am in bed, all I can think about is how wonderful it would be to have your nude body snuggled up close to me. Yes, Angela, I am in love with you. However, I wish that I was not. Sometimes I wish we had never met. I will try to explain. There is about 16 year's difference in our ages. That is not too difficult. I have two teen aged children. I think we could find a way to live with that. You would likely want to work. How would you handle that knowing that I work as a contractor? My jobs last a few months to a year or some times a year and a half. I work about half of the time. When I work it is usually very long hours, ten to sixteen hours a day, plus eight or ten on Saturday. My children are in boarding school part of the year. During school vacations they go with me."

She said, "I didn't ask you to marry me. I just wondered why we don't see more of each other now."

"Because a serious relationship is the only kind I could have with you. As much as I enjoyed being with you, it has something missing. Don't get me wrong. I enjoyed every minute with you in bed. You said you were a virgin and you wanted to stay that way. I promised you would. And you did. However;

That left me hurting. So I must avoid a reoccurrence for my health's sake."

"Kirk, I want to make it clear to you. After being in bed with you and the things we did, I loved every minute of it. I have changed my mind about maintaining my virginity. I want to share my life with you.

I want to express my love for you in every possible way that I can."

"Thank you. I could not do that. I love you too much. It would hurt if I had sexual intercourse with you, and a few weeks later you are having it with someone else. If we were planning to marry, then I could cheat a few months or years and have a complete love/sex relationship. But, I think you can see that marriage is not practical."

"Marriage is not practical now, next week, or even next year. We need to get to know each other a lot better. As far as age difference, your children, your work schedule, all of those things sound interesting, even fun. If you asked today for me to marry you, I would say, "no". The adjustment to each other will take time. I don't want to be rushed and I don't want you to feel rushed."

"You have a lot of maturity for your age."

"I never thought, I would have to beg any man for sex; but, will you please go to bed and have sex with me right now?"

"No! If we are to make love to each other, it will have to be done right, starting in the living room."

We got up from the table and I went into the living room. She stayed behind to clean of the table and start the dish washer. Well, I thought, keeping a neat apartment must be very important to her. I liked that.

"Excuse me Kirk. Make yourself comfortable, I will be right back."

She disappeared down the hall. After a few minutes she reappeared, wearing a shear night gown with nothing on under it. She stood there about ten feet away from me, and said, "I have, as you know, never made love with anyone. The closest I have come was that night in bed with you. However, I have read and I believe I understand what you expect of me. I thought it important for you to understand that. OK?"

"OK! Now come over here and sit on my lap."

She must have read a lot of books on sexual performance because she was an expert at every aspect. We worked at it slowly. When I kissed her lips, I felt her hot tongue. I opened her night gown and looked at those beautiful breasts. Felt them with my hands, kissed them, licked them and sucked on them. I raised her off my lap, stood in front of her, and dropped my pants and shorts, to rub my penis across her breasts. Before I could, she got her hand around it and kissed it, then put it in her mouth. After a few minutes, I pulled it out and sat back down on the couch beside her and gestured for her to sit on me facing me. Her knees were folded on each side of me. She was moist inside and I entered her with ease.

I said, "Let's go to bed."

I finished getting undressed, and she removed her night gown. I noticed that the blanket and top sheet were already pulled back. We lay down and we started all over again, kissing, licking, sucking and I put my tongue to work as I did at our first encounter at my house. She liked to look at my penis. Then quickly, she jumped off of the bed, went into the bath room and came back with a pan of water, a wash cloth, and a towel. She carefully washed and dried my penis. Then in her mouth again.

Then I got on top of her, put it in then raised her legs onto my shoulders. I grasped both legs in my hands and raised her up and down a few inches. I heard her climax. I laid down on her once again and ejaculated.

We lay side by side, relaxed and enervated. We turned and faced each other. She reached down and put my soft penis against her pubic hair.

I wondered, is high sexual motivation a sin? Can anything this beautiful be wrong? A person with low sexual motivation would likely say it is a sin, it is wrong, and those people involved are going to hell.

At her front door, I kissed her and hugged her, I wanted, never to let go.

She said, with tears running down her cheeks, "Are you sure you want to leave."

"I don't want to; But, I must leave paradise and get back to the other part of life."

CHAPTER 14

Monday morning my ad was running, and the phone started ringing early. This time I did not interview many. The third caller said, "I am 5 feet 3 inches, blond, blue eyes, 22 years old. Since she did not have transportation, I went to her apartment for the interview. She passed. I hired her. We gathered her stuff and moved her back to my house.

My phone was ringing so I asked her to wait in the living room. On the phone was a man responding to my ad. He wanted to know if I would take a "fella". I told him yes; But, I had already filled the position. The phone was ringing again, and someone was knocking at the front door. I yelled at my new house keeper to answer it. This phone call was obviously from a black man.

He wanted to know if I would take an African American woman. I said, "I certainly would since I am an African American myself."

I went back in the living room to find Bryan was the door knocker. He was getting acquainted with Delores as I walked in he asked her,

She seemed nervous when saying, "I am going to work for Kirk."

"Oh, what are you going to do for Kirk?"

"House keeper."

I interrupted, "That is enough Bryan. Knock it off before you scare the girl away. So when did you get back in town. I can't remember where you were going or what you were going to do."

"I have been in Las Vegas selling hearing aids. I fitted one girl in her pussy so she could hear her boyfriend cum."

"There you go again, Bryan. I think it is time for you to leave."

After Bryan left, I asked Delores if she would like a mixed drink. She said no. But that did not stop me. I had a couple of drinks and I asked if she would like to go out for dinner. I wanted to get her off to a good start.

After we got back home, I had a few more drinks. I sat beside her, put my arm around her, kissed her, and reached for a one of her very big breasts. She didn't try to stop me until I ran my hand up her leg.

She said, "No don't."

I said, "Why. What is the problem?"

"You move your hand up a little further, and you will find out."

"No thanks. I'll keep my hand off you. Are you about ready to go to bed?"

"Where do you want me to sleep?"

"With me, of course."

I stripped and jumped into bed. She was just a few minutes behind me. I extended my arm onto her pillow. And she put her head on it. I kissed her a few times and sucked on those big tits. I jumped up and straddled her chest, put my prick between her tits and squeezed the tits together. I lay back on my back, got one hand under her neck, lifted her head and brought it back down on my prick. She opened her mouth just in time. It did not take long. I ejaculated in her mouth. She quickly swallowed it.

I asked, "Would you like a glass of water or anything else."

"Water would be nice."

I gave her a drink of water, and suggested, "You go to sleep. I am going in the living room for a while"

I phoned Angela. Thanked her for the good time Sunday, and told her that I loved her.

* * *

Tuesday just before noon, I went into the bank that had most of my accounts. Two young ladies working at desks near the entry stopped their work long enough to give me very inviting looks. The first one, I had met a couple of times before. She sat next to a male loan officer that I knew quite well. I stood next to his desk, waiting for him to finish the phone call that he was on. While waiting, the young woman next to him spoke kind of to herself but loud enough for me to hear, "I don't know what I am going to do during my lunch period."

I heard, but acted as if I had not. She was married, cheated on her husband every chance she got. She had a beautiful pair of legs, nicely tanned, and she did her best to show them off. She was pretty all over except bucked teeth. I thought to myself how it would not be pleasant to kiss, and how dangerous to let her blow me.

The loan officer finished his phone call and we had a nice conversation. Before I walked away he said, "Let me introduce you to our new employee. Claudia, this is Mister Donaldson."

"I am happy to meet you sir,"

Jeff went back to his desk, leaving us alone. I said, "Claudia have you had lunch yet."

"No. I was just leaving."

"I will walk you to your car, if that is OK."

As we approached her car, I said, "Could I take you to lunch?"

She said, "I would like to; But, I have to go home and fix lunch for my husband. Next time, don't forget to ask me again."

This statement should have awakened me. She was married; but that didn't dampen her interest in other men. I had been living a questionable life. I had stopped attending church regularly and was living generally a non-Christian life. However, I had not gotten so low that I would date a married woman.

* * *

My daughter was home from school for a week. She brought her friend, Jan, to the house for a visit. Jan was 16, almost 17. She was divorced from a 'shot gun marriage'; we called it when I was a young man. She had gotten pregnant when barely 15. She married the father of the baby. A few months later she started divorce proceedings. Her mother took care of the baby most of the time.

The girls were leaving. Donnelda (my Daughter) kissed me good bye, and to my surprise so did Jan. They returned in less than an hour.

Donnelda told me, "Jan liked kissing you and it was not like kissing an older man."

Donnelda had to go pick up my house keeper. She asked, " Jan, I will only be gone a couple of hours. You stay and entertain my dad."

Jan looked very pleased, smiled and said, "OK."

I felt sure, they had discussed this arrangement.

I guess I will never understand women. Jan was so young. She seemed to know just about nothing about sex. She was about five feet, seven inches tall; I guess she weighed about 105 pounds, slender, a flat stomach with stretch marks, small breasts with large nipples. She liked my weight on her. She just lay flat on her back with a smile on her face. When I finished, she said, "That was nice."

I was in the bank about a week later. Claudia saw me walk in, held up a hand and motioned with her finger. She gave me a big smile and asked me to sit. That looked better if anyone in the bank questioned my being there. She said, "I can go to lunch with you any time. My husband and I separated and we are getting a divorce."

We had lunch together. That evening we went to Griffith Park for an evening climb of the mountain. She was 22 years old. I held hands with her during much of the walk. When we finished and got back into my car, I kissed her. It took a lot of nerve for me to do that. I think our age difference concerned me. When we got back to her apartment she invited me in. We sat on her couch with her pit bull between us. She told me later that was for protection.

I took her to a cocktail party put on by the San Fernando Valley Republican party. She told me that was her first cocktail party. At her apartment she again invited me in, then immediately excused herself, went in to the bed room and came out wearing a robe, with bear feet. I don't know what happened to the pit bull. It was nice to have nothing between us.

Claudia was about the hottest female I had ever met. In bed, she asked me, "What can I do that will really turn you on?"

I guess I didn't get excited enough to suit her. I said, "Lick my balls."

She didn't just lick them. She sucked each one into her mouth.

At this point, I have to say, I am glad that I use fictitious names to write this book. Otherwise, she may want to kill me or put a law suit against me.

* * *

My house keeper went with me to Don's house one evening. Don had a beautiful house in an exclusive part of Northridge. He lived with a girl that he had met in **PWS** and her four year old daughter. After we talked enough to feel we had gotten acquainted, we went into the back yard. Don and his girlfriend stripped and got in the pool. I followed and Delores was immediately after me. After the pool playing we sat in a circle facing each other. Don spread the legs of his girl and started working on her between her legs with his mouth. I put my penis in Delores' mouth and then in her between her legs. Quickly, I had her legs around me and I was in a squatted position with her weight and mine on my feet. I heard Don saying, "We have to try that sometime.

We went into the house and finished the evening watching some of Don's pornographic movies.

* * *

An attorney friend phoned to tell me that his wife left him and filed for divorce.

I told him, "Fred, You called the right person. Have you heard of **PWS**?"

"No can't say that I have."

After explaining **PWS**, I told him, "They are having a party tonight; I will pick you up at seven."

Driving to the party, I heard the complete story about his separation and less than successful marriage. He was a very good looking man and his wife that I had met only once was just plain ugly. She had worked to put him through law school. As we approached the party house, I told Fred, "If you get a girl lined up before I do, and she has a car, and she is willing to take you after the party, let me know. That will free me to take a chick in my car. Now if I get one before you do, I will hand you the keys to my car and go in the lady's car. That leaves you responsible for my car. Please park it in front of your house with the keys on top of the front left tire. Do you understand all of that?"

"Yes. I think so. One question, you seem very sure that at least one of us will get a female."

"Believe me Fred, I am sure."

In the foyer of the house, I introduced Fred. He got a little paper badge with his name on it. As we walked from the foyer toward the living room, I spotted a glassy eyed, well stacked chick staring at me. She was sitting on a couch in the rather large foyer. I reached down with both hands. She took both of my hands and got up. I said, "Are you ready to leave?"

"Yes."

Fred looked at us, no doubt believing that we knew each other. I handed my car key to him.

When we got to her car, she handed the key to me. Inside I put both arms around her and gave her a big kiss. She said, "You know, don't you?"

"Yes, I know."

She immediately started playing with my prick through my pants. So to facilitate her before driving away, I got it out for her. We went directly to my house. Fortunately Delores was visiting with a friend and would not be back until about seven AM.

I had very good control at that time in my life. She kept working hard while I drove the approximately seven miles. We went directly to my bed when we got there. She worked it back and forth between her mouth and her legs with no washing it in between.

After about two hours, I suggested we go get something to eat. As I drove her car a few miles to a restaurant, she never took it out of her mouth. We arrived. I parked the car and asked, "Are you ready to get something to eat?"

She said, "I already had something to eat."

I was hungry. I ate a big breakfast. She had a cup of coffee. We had our first opportunity to just talk. She shocked me when she said, "I was not legal at that **PWS** party because I am married."

This statement caused me to think. My x-wife was sexually cold and she cheated on me. I thought she was trying

to find the great sexual thrills and excitement that she be-
lieved should be a natural part of sex. But I have run in
to some really hot women that are divorced. I thought, be-
cause their x-husbands went looking as Bonnie had done?
Could be.

I never asked why she was screwing a stranger instead of her husband. She told me about her employment, which was supervisor over a group of women that did telephone soliciting for direct sales companies. She let me know also that she was an atheist. My opinion of this female was going down rather rapidly.

I phoned her once when I was about to come home from a business trip. I asked if she would like to meet me at my house. I was a few thousand miles away. I figured from when the plane was due to land, and how much time would be required for a taxi to drive me from LAX to my home. The calculated time of arrival was just right for the time she got off work.

The problem was the plane was late landing, and I misjudged the time to pick up my luggage. Lili ended up waiting an hour and a half in my front yard.

We took a shower together. She spent an hour and a half doing her usual performance. As we lay panting, I suggested to her "My friend, Fred, the attorney is lonely since splitting with his wife, and you would be well thought of if you would keep him company once in a while."

Her reaction was immediate, "Listen Kirk. You can put it in anywhere you like; but don't ask me to take care of your friends."

* * *

The next morning I received a phone call from Harold Morris. "Good morning Harold."

"Good morning Kirk. I hope you are doing well. I'll tell you the reason I call. It is very important. How would you like to be on television?"

"Frankly, it doesn't excite me. Why. What do you have in mind?"

"Current Broadcast System is going to do a special show on the lives of divorced people. It will be broadcast prime time, Sunday night at about 9:00 PM. They have asked **PWS** for about 10 people to answer questions about their lives after divorce."

"That sounds like fun. Depending on when they want to record I would like to be included. Thanks for asking me."

* * *

I felt like I had been too busy. I needed a rest, or at least a change. I asked Delores, "Would you like to go camping at one of the national parks for a few days?"

"Yes. Which one?"

"How about Sequoia? Think you would like that one?

"Yes. Daddy has a camper that we could put on your pick up to sleep in."

"Great. I usually sleep in my sleeping bag in a tent. However, a camper sounds great."

We went to her dad's house and loaded the camper on my pick up.

The next morning, we pulled out a little after five AM. Drove to Fresno. Parked in a residential neighborhood. Climbed up in the overhead where I enjoyed playing with her beautiful big tits. She introduced something new, or at least it was new to me, she stopped sucking, then worked her head under my balls and put her tongue in my rectum.

Where dose a 22 year old learn things like this?

I was there for a rest. But it appeared that I was not going to get one.

CHAPTER 15

I am going to tell you about four of the unmarried women that I met in my church. They are the only woman from my church that I had any contact with outside of the church:

Woman A

My church had a Sunday school class just for un-married and singles. The class was usually attended by about 150 people. That is 90 women and 60 men would be a close guess. I was chairman of the board of trustees and had the responsibility for all of the buildings. As such, I would often stand and observe.

One morning I stood in the narthex just outside the Singles Sunday School (SSS) class. A fit and proper woman about 35 to 40 years old that had been a member of the church for many years was exiting the class. I hardly knew her. She stopped to say hello. I guess she knew that Bonnie and I had split. To my surprise she looked right into my eyes and said, "Would you like to come over for dinner tonight?"

"I don't get very many invitations for good home cooking. I accept. What time?"

"6 PM. Is that OK?"

"I'll see you at six."

I looked up her address in the church directory. Driving there, I thought *this will be a special evening, one without sex.*

She came to the door with shorts and a halter top. I had seen her many times; But, Always with a dress. I stepped in and gave her a brief hug. She had a beautiful home, well furnished, about 3,000 square feet. She directed me to the living room. We had a lot of conversation, all about the church.

She surprised me when she told me about the Pastor.

"I have been the substitute secretary, and the regular secretary is a close friend of mine. There are a few women that have regular weekly appointments with the Pastor. They go in his office. He closes the door, and tells Grace or me to hold all calls, and don't disturb him for an hour. When the ladies leave their hair is messy, and so with their makeup. They are sweaty. No doubt what they had been doing."

I said, "This is shocking."

"I am sorry. I didn't mean to shock you. Are you ready to eat? It is ready."

We had roast duck, sweet potatoes and a salad. "A fine meal", I said.

"Would you like desert now or a little later?"

"That depends on what you have in mind for us to do and how long it will take to do it."

"Well, I do have something in mind. How big are you around the waist?"

"About 34 inches. Why?"

"I have a pair of trunks for you to wear with me in my hot tub."

I said, "That sounds like fun, relaxing fun."

In the hot tub we sat on a bench. Soon after we were in she turned and put her legs across my lap. She moved them a little closer to my stomach. I was sure that she could tell that I had an erection. I took both hands and moved her legs off of me. She looked surprised and I thought disappointed. However she didn't realize that I did it so that I could get closer to her. I moved in very close, put my arm across her shoulders. She immediately leaned forward so my arm could go much lower down. She turned her face toward me. I planted a big kiss on her lips. I pushed her a little more forward, and with both hands behind her back, I untied her halter. I did a little kissing of her small breasts.

She was moving her arms in such a way that she felt my erection several times. Then suddenly she sat up straight and said, "Kirk, I have to tell you something. It is my time of the month. I am having my period."

Woman B

I went to the Tuesday night Bible study group. It was for SSS people, and was taught by a married man. After the study period we had a social time. I met a woman who was about 25 years old. I had seen her before: But, Had never spoken to her.

We conversed for half an hour. She had an unusual back ground. She was raised Roman Catholic,. I walked her to her car. She said, "I live just a few blocks from here. You can follow me if you like."

"I'll do that."

She had a very small apartment. . When I went in she offered to make a cup of coffee or whatever I wanted. While she was making the hot drink, I sat on the sofa.

When she brought it into me, she set in on the coffee table in front of me. She asked me to move over to the middle of the sofa. I didn't know why; But, I did it without question. Then she sat beside me with her legs across my legs. No slacks. A dress that came up to the middle of her upper legs. I would have been uncomfortable to not have put my hands on her bare legs.

I went on ahead and had sex with her even though she had a very bad problem. Oder! She was a heavy smoker that smelled and she smelled at the other end like fish that had been out of the refrigerator for a week.

This person and this story reminded me of something that happened after a Bible study from another church.

Woman C

I was standing in the narthex when the SSS was over. A woman that I had never seen before was slowly exiting. She was good looking, about 30 years old, and she had what I call that unmistakable sexy look about her. I put on my "director of the church" act and asked, did you like our class?" I dodged a little to one side and she moved with me and stopped. I less than five minutes, I had her phone number and a tentative meeting time for that evening.

That evening when I kncked at her door, I expected to be asked in. Instead she welded out. I didn't ask why. I suggested we go to a restaurant or my house. She chose the restaurant.

We each had a cup of coffee with our conversation. She was a grammar school teacher, and had two daughters. I estimate we were in the restaurant 20 minutes. She rather bluntly said, "Let's go to your house."

At my house we sat side by side. Wasting no time, we started kissing immediately. Feeling her breast, I noticed something felt strange. She gave an explanation, namely that she had surgery a few years past and what I felt was a plastic implant. It was not long until she removed her blouse. I removed my pants and shorts, and she started sucking. When I reached the point where I was about to ejaculate, I pulled it out, thinking she would object if I did it in her mouth. To the contrary, she said, "I'd like you to keep on doing it."

She did. I did. Hard to believe that I just met her that morning at SSS.

I thought I was just about where I could classify the sexual make up of the American female.

Looks; *If one is very good looking she has more offers and thus gets more experience. Ever hear a fat, ugly one say, I don't allow men to mess around with my body. Who would want to?*

Woman D

This woman I did not meet at church. Rather, I met her at a singles night at the shopping mall (after all of the stores close). However, she was a member and regular attendee at my church. A few minutes of conversation and I followed her to her house. She was a school teacher. I thought of the old story, if a teacher is not pleased with the way you did it, she will make you do it over and over. She must have liked the way I did it because she didn't make me do it over again. It was conventional, like we had been married for ten years. The church was having classes every Wednesday evening. The sub-ject was something to do with raising children. She described her girlfriend that would be at the class, and suggested that I say hello.

Woman E

I met her outside the church during intermission. She was smoking. I know, I said it before; but, I am going to say it again. This was the hottest woman I had ever met. The class that I met her in was, *Caring for children after divorce.* She had two. She was a conscientious house keeper and mother. She was a member of the church and attended regularly.

She had a perfect figure and beautiful skin. There was only one negative thing that I could say about her, she smoked.

I recognized her from the description given me by her friend. I got her address in class and her preference for wine. On the way to her house, I bought a liter bottle of wine. We sat at her kitchen table and drank the whole bottle. She told me, of course, what a son of a bitch her x was.

I tried kissing her a few times at the table. She pushed me away each time, not like she didn't want me to; But because she knew that if she let something get started she would not be able to stop until she had gotten complete sexual satisfaction.

I went to her rest room. Upon my return she was sitting on the sofa. I thought she had given up.

She didn't push me away anymore. She did let me know she was mistrusting. As we hugged and kissed the heat was building in both of us. She climaxed, wow what a noise. It was obvious that she was not going to remove her under pants so I unzipped my pants, took them off in front of her, and she knew what to do.

Are Christianity and sexual motivation opposite? I don't think so. The opposite is very likely true. The five women that I just described are active Members of the body of Christ. I believe that a really warm woman would likely agree. The cold women more likely would say these five women are Sluts and should be ashamed to step foot in church. I have known women in the church that can't remember their premarital sexual activity.

I am going to give you a list of people in the bible who were less than

Perfect ;
Noah was a drunk
Abraham was too old
Isaac was a daydreamer
Jacob was a liar
Leah was ugly
Joseph was abused
Moses had a stuttering problem
Sampson was a womanizer
Rehab was a prostitute
Jeremiah & Timothy; too young

David had an affair and murdered
Elijah was suicidal
Isaiah preached naked
Jonah ran from god
Naomi was a widow
Job went bankrupt
John the Baptist ate bugs
Peter denied Christ
The disciples slipped while praying
Martha worried about everything
The Samaritan woman was divorced
Zachariah was too small
Timothy had an ulcer
Lazarus was dead
Gideon was afraid

* * *

I received a phone call from Don. He wanted to know if I would be interested in going with him and his live in girlfriend to a nudist camp near Riverside. He explained, "We have to go as couples."

I told him, "I will have to think about it. I'll call you back tomorrow and let you know." I felt sure that I could make it; But, What female would I take along. Delores, my house keeper, I think she would like to go. So I went in the den where she was reading and asked, "My friend, Don, and his girlfriend are going to a nudist camp out near Riverside. He has asked if we would like to go with them. I told him, I would check with you and let him know tomorrow."

She looked like she was seriously thinking about it, "I would have to know something about the place. Is it for families or could I be raped."

"I'll phone Don back and ask when he could talk to us about it."

"OK. That sounds good to me."

A few minutes later I returned to the den, "I talked to Don. We can go over there after dinner tonight.

He and his girlfriend were nude when they let us in. He led our way to the living room. His girlfriend offered coffee or a soft drink.

I spoke up and said, "OK, Don fill us in."

The camp is comprised of about ten acres. It has two swimming pools. A well-equipped exercise facility, a restaurant with inside and outside dining, several concessions, and an RV park for full time or at least long term guests."

I asked, "Are there any restrictions as far as admittances go."

"Yes. Couples only, or couples with children. No touching."

"Delores, What do you say? Do you have anything to ask?"

"No, I am ready to go."

When we all met for the drive to the camp, I was surprised that an engineer that I had worked with and his wife were going with us.

I took my truck because I had learned the roads in the camp were dirt, and also because Delores fathers camper was still on it. When we got there, a line was waiting to go in. We took advantage of the wait and by the time we were at the check in, we were both nude. We drove by several trailers and tents getting to our parking place. After we were parked, we took a walk around the grounds. I saw so many Orientals that I asked a passerby. She said they were Japanese Television people filming a documentary. We past one concession that was a barber, another was a beauty shop; another was a woman piercing ears. There must have been a couple of hundred people lying beside the big pool. The teen agars seem to enjoy themselves. . A beautiful one about sixteen walked by us with a large beach towel around her neck and falling down partially covering her breasts. That partly covered condition was more attractive than complete nudity in my opinion. A man,

Darwin would like to have seen, walked by. His entire body was covered with hair.

Being there caused me to believe the Japanese have the right idea. They do not associate nudity with sex. They have bath houses were everyone is nude; Men and women use the same rest rooms or adjacent rest rooms with walk thru one to get to the other.

I observed one woman that had been lying completely nude by the pool, got up walked to her car, and got dressed. She forgot something and walked back to the place where she had been laying, bent over to pick it up, and three men raised up to see a small part of her breast as her blouse gapped open.

If she had come back nude no one would have looked at her.

Delores and I walked back to the camper. When we got in I was suddenly sexually aroused. Not because we had been walking around the nude people outside. We went right to making love. A nap arm in arm with those beautiful big tits against me.

A nock on the door. It was Don, "Are you guys about ready to go to dinner."

I opened the door and asked him, "How should we dress for dinner."

"This is a come as you are dinner."

After lining up for dinner, we sat at a long table with four other people. Everyone was friendly. We discussed the Japanese film makers, the food that was very satisfying, and church. These people were like the majority of Americans, that is they spoke respectfully about churches, and people who attend them, and they believe Jesus must have been a nice person. They think if there is an afterlife, they will certainly be welcomed because they have lived good lives.

A few days later, I went into a bank, lined up, and when I was first in line, I took a close look at the teller as she did at me. "I have seen you somewhere before..… Now I know." I moved close to her ear and said, "I recognized you even with your clothes on."

She smiled.

* * *

I phoned Angela Saturday afternoon. "And how is my love today?"

"I am lonely Kirk."

"You know, I have a house keeper now. That could affect our activities in my house."

"She has no effect on activities in my apartment. Where have you been? I phoned you a couple of times in the past few days."

"I had to go out of town, negotiating a contract for work. This happens often."

"Did you get the job?"

"No. They don't happen that fast."

"Would you like to come over for dinner?"

"I have a better idea. How would it be if I came over for church and breakfast tomorrow?"

"I have a better, better idea. Bring your church cloths and your tooth brush, and come over for dinner."

"You know, I can't say, "No". I will see you in an hour."

She met me at the door. Shorts, a tea shirt, bear feet, and beautiful as ever.

Obviously nothing on under the tea shirt. I could see her nipples.

"Come in Kirk."

"You look eatable."

"Right now I am going to pass on that statement. Have a seat in the living room. And, what would you like to drink.

"Water would be nice. Did your friends get back from Israel?"

"Yes. Yesterday."

"Would you still like to go? I mean, would you like to go with me?"

"You are kidding with me. Aren't you Kirk?"

"No. I am not kidding. I am so very much in love with you."

"Do you mean get married, and then go?"

"I thought that you would be thrilled and excided with the thought of going to the Holy Land."

"I am thrilled. I am excited. But, many things must be considered."

"I agree, and it is time to start considering. First you must drop all of your old boy friends."

"Ha. That is funny. Right now I am going to sit on your lap and let you know how much I love you."

"Would you get up for just a minute? I have to readjust something before you break it off."

She rose up. I reached down into my pants for a moment and she sat back down.

"I hope I did not injure it. I may need it after dinner."

She came on with many beautiful kisses. I could not stand to have her on my lap without feeling and touching. She could sense that, and got up and soon announced that dinner was ready.

She was a very good cook. It was an all vegetable meal.

After dinner we sat across the room from each other. We both knew this was the only way we could have a conversation. No feel. No touch. No kiss. Just talk.

We discussed my children, and the fact that I could never make her pregnant. We talked about our age difference. We talked about everything except my alcohol problem. I believed that I could stop drinking anytime.

She asked, "When do I get to meet your children."

"Next week. Now I am getting a little sleepy. What will your neighbors think if they know that I stayed all night with you?"

"I hadn't thought about it. We have been talking for over two hours. May I come over there and sit with you now."

"Yes! Please get that beautiful body over here. Enough of that serious talk."

We made love for hours. One thing I can say for sure, "Sex is much better when it is with someone I love." I asked her, "Do you think that we will ever get tired of making love ?"

"I don't think so".

In the morning, we showered together. I so enjoyed washing that beautiful body all over.

* * *

At church, I wondered if the pastor had seen my car parked in front of Angela's apartment. His sermon was about trying to keep our sins hidden from God. "It is sure that your sin will find you out. Numbers 32:23. We may be able to hide our sins from people around us, but nothing is ever hidden from God. Hebrews 4:13. He sees each of our thoughts, failures, and motivations. Luke 12:2-3, 1 Samuel 16:7. If we confess our sins, God is faithful and just to forgive our sins and to cleanse us from unrighteousness. 1John 1:9. So don't let unconfused sins come between you and God."

I looked at Angela a few times. She seem to be a little upset. Leaving the church, the pastor was at the middle door. That is the door that Angela normally used. This morning, she chose another door to avoid the pastor.

Angela had nothing to say as we approached the car. I held the door for her, and then quickly went around. As I got in I put an arm around her, saying, "That sermon got to you, didn't it."

"Yes it did", She replied.

"Where do you want to eat?"

"Kirk, please take me home, and I'll phone you later."

* * *

The next night I went volley ball as was my usual Monday night habit. Angela had not phoned last night as I expected she would. I know that that sermon really got to her. Does that mean no more sex? That was hard to believe with her motivation. She may want to break up with me because she knows that being around her would be difficult for me if there was no sex. Of course she believed that all the sex that I got was from her. A thought crossed my mind. *If Angela and I were married could I give up other sex partners and be true to her alone ?*

Buck and Len were moving my way. "Kirk, are you going to play, or stand there day dreaming all night."

"I think I will just stand here and day dream as you call it."

Len said, "There is only one thing that could cause Kirk to miss a game of volley ball, and that is pussy. Who is she Kirk?"

I don't think Len or Buck ever had a serious moment thinking about a female. To both of them, females are just a places to put penises.

Buck and Len had a lot in common, namely, they both believed that women are for screwing and nothing else. They both wanted to be married; But, to whom? Not to the women they had been screwing. Buck came up with an idea. He ran an ad in the capitol city of a Central American country. The ad read something like this, *'Handsome, rich, American seeks a wife, She must be under 20 years old, virgin, and ready to relocate to the United States. Interview will be in the lobby of (a hotel named)(date). Some English helpful.'* "Under 20", Len was about 40. The hotel lobby was over flowing with females dressed in their Sunday best. After eight hours, Len picked one. And married her the next morning. He met all of her family during the next two days. The bride and groom stayed in the hotel where Len took her virginity. This is what Len wanted. A beautiful young virgin. "Nothing like those cheap whores he had been screwing back in the states." He gave her an airline ticket and let her stay a few days while she finished getting a past port. A few days later he went to a U S Port of entry to get her, only to learn that she had been denied entry, and sent back because she was 17 years old. Len never seem to have a guilty conscious for having nearly ruined that young girl's life. She would find it very difficult or impossible to find a man that would have her after being married and divorced from an American.

Buck believed that Len generally had good ideas. He tried a little different version. He ran a similar ad in a large city in the Philippines. Had about the same results. Picked a beautiful 20 year old virgin, married her and brought her home with him. The last time I talked to him he said every thing was great. I asked about sex. His reply was, "She chases me around the house."

Len followed Buck's example and is happily (he said) married to a Philippine girl. I can remember having two German girlfriends. The problem was communication. They both treated me like I was a king. Give me an American girl anytime.

Rebecca had been playing. She saw me, politely left the game and came over with a big "hello".

"Hello Rebecca. How have you been?"

"Fine; But, I will have to admit, I have missed you, Kirk".

"What are you doing after volley ball ?"

"Nothing. What do you have in mine?" With a cute little smile.

"Come up to my house and we will see if we can find something to do."

"OK. I am sure we will find something, and I believe I know what that something will be. I am ready to leave."

She seemed like the same old Rebecca. As soon as she got in the house, she started fingering my pants. I stopped her for a moment and removed her blouse and bra so I would have something to play with while she sucked my cock. I made it a clean shot, all in her mouth. She loved it; But not as much as she would have like it if I had shot it all over her face.

We sat down in the den for a few minutes just looked at each other. She seems to have something serious on her mind.

She asked, "Kirk, You have had sex with other women recently, right ?"

"What is this are you writing a book ? Surely you are not jealous ?"

"I think I can assume, yes, you have. In fact probably several different women. Now, the reason that I asked. I met a man in PWS. He seemed to be very nice. After I got to know him, I thought really well, we had sex."

"How long did it take to get to know him. Ten minutes or Fifteen? I am sorry. Go on with your story."

"I am pregnant. I need an abortion. It cost three hundred and fifty dollars. He gave me fifty dollars and vanished. He knew about you. He asked me if you could be the father. I explained to him that you had surgery and were unable to get anybody pregnant. I need to borrow three hundred dollars."

"Try a bank."

I never saw Rebecca again.

I did hear that she married one of the guys from the club. I knew him fairly well. He had custody of his two children. He was an outspoken atheist, overweight, and I doubt if he had had a woman in the last few years. He had been dating Rebecca while she was still seeing me. I remember on afternoon she phoned me asking to be near her house at 10:30 PM when Bob would bring her home. She told me that she had told him all about me. Finally he took her to Las Vegas. He rented a fancy room, had sex with her and asked her to marry him. What she wanted was a step father for her children. I heard a few months later that they had split.

I wandered how is one person to pick another for marriage when about 50% end up in divorce. From what I have been able to observe, the couples that are most likely to stay together until death are older when they get married and are active members of a fundamentalist church. They have been saved. They each already accept Christ and his teaching and they accept each other as they are.

CHAPTER 16

The big day came. That is, I am supposed to believe it to be a big day. We all met at the television studio. We were to film Saturday afternoon for a show that was to appear at nine PM on a Sunday night. The subject was, "Surviving Divorce". There were about 12 of us. The Master of Ceremonies was a very popular TV star. The strange thing was he was not there. The so called writer of the show sat in front of our group and asked the questions. Clair Norman was in our group. She had a master's degree in psychology and was well on the way to a doctor. I had only three semesters of psychology many years before. Guess which one of us had almost everything said, cut. You guessed it, Clair. The answers she gave were so intelligent the TV people did not want them. I said what they wanted to hear. I talked like a dummy. When I was asked to summaries, I said, "If I had known years earlier what I know now, I would have divorced much earlier. The first week of my newly found freedom, I learned about PARANTS WITHOUT SPOUCES. I went to an orientation meeting got immediately involved, met a room full of lovely women, and got invited to a party and to play volley ball the following week. I learned in the first few weeks that the birth control pill had emancipated women. I also learned that they enjoy sex as much as or more than men. My ex-spouse had me convinced that her coldness was normal and that I was nuts to still want sex after ten years of marriage." When the show aired the MC was there and we were in a different room. How did they do that ?

* * *

I phoned Angela to tell her that I had landed a very good contract a couple of hundred miles away. It should last a few weeks. It was not true. I just needed time without her to think. The relationship was getting too serious. I believed I could hear her crying.

She said, "Do we have to say good bye on the telephone."

"No. Do you want me to come over?"

"Yes"

"And how late do you want me to stay?" Remembering how that sermon had affected her.

"I want you to stay all night, all week, all year. I love you Kirk."

"Can I take you out to dinner?"

"I'll cook here."

"No. This time, I am going to be the boss. I will be there in an hour. Be ready and I am going to take you out to dinner."

When I arrived, she opened the door and I froze. She was beautiful. I put out my arms and she stepped between them. We just stood there for the longest time, not caring weather neighbors or anyone else could see us, holding each other tightly.

Finally I said, "Are you ready to go?"

She just nodded her head.

The waiter asked, "Table or Booth"

Angela quickly answered. "Booth".

She sat on my right. Fortunately, I am ambidextrous. We sat so close that while she ate with her right hand and I ate with my left hand.

Back at her apartment she excused herself and left the room. However before leaving she suggested that I consider taking off all of my clothing. I decided not to remove my clothing.

When she returned, she was completely nude. She asked, "Do you feel uncomfortable with all of those cloths on."

"Yes I do. I want you to remove them."

She enjoyed every piece that she slowly removed.

We enjoyed sex in just about every way that it could be enjoyed.

In the morning, I kissed her good bye about 10 times. I really hated to go. And she really hated to see me go. How could I be so in love with such a wonderful woman and lie to her? I told her that I would phone her, and be back as soon as the job is complete. Also, I reminded her, "Give some thought to Israel and marriage."

She quickly said, "I don't need to think about it, I am ready to go to Israel and I am ready to marry you."

* * *

Delores was at the door when she heard the car. She seemed to be a little angry. Of course, I knew why. She considered herself more than just a house keeper. She was living full time with me, sleeping with me, having sex with me. When I would stay out all night, she of course believed that I was with a female. Different from all of the other female friends that I had, I did not lie to Delores. She was to cook, keep the house clean, go with me on an occasional camping trip, and if she wanted, she could go to bed with me. If she didn't want any of these, plenty of others did want them.

She said, "Art Commings had called. He wants you to call him. It is rather serious. It concerns me."

"What do you mean, it concerns you. You have never met Art,"

"I was on the phone with him for about an hour this morning. Please phone him. He will explain."

I phoned him. He explained. He and Delores had fallen in love on the phone. They agreed that they would like to live together. With my permission, he would be up to move her stuff in half an hour.

"OK Art. Come and get her", I said.

Art and I had gone to church together. He was well off financially, owned his own business, and had a beautiful home in Woodland Hills. His wife left him about the same time that mine left. He left our church and joined a Mormon church after he had been told that Mormon women would be much more to his liking.

* * *

Claudia had moved from her apartment. She now lived in a small house in the back yard of a Los Angeles County Deputy Sheriff. I phoned her about 9 o'clock. She quickly used one of my old tricks, i.e., "I don't like to talk on the phone. Why don't you come over?"

"I'll be right there."

Driving to her house, I wondered if any physical problems could arise from having too much sex.

When I arrived, she was wearing a short, see through night gown.

"Come in Kirk. Are you ready to go to bed?"

"I am not sleepy. But, I am ready to go to bed"

"Here it is. I'll join you in a few minutes. Don't go to sleep."

I could hear the shower running.

When she jumped in bed she immediately started sucking my cock, and licking balls. She knew just when to stop to avoid my ejaculating in her mouth.

I am sure that she wanted me to lick her between her legs. I could not because she smelled down there like dead fish.

The next night she came to my house. I prepared a rotisserie chicken and vegetables. She thought I cooked the chicken from scratch. I just let her think that.

We showered together. Then with the blankets pulled back we laid on my king sized bed. I sucked on her tit just a little until she told me that they were too sensitive. I kissed her body all over, almost, avoiding her smelly area. She had another smelly area. Her mouth always smelled like peanut butter.

With her lying on her back, I sat on her chest with my erection in her mouth. After about ten minutes of this, I could feel it coming on. I said, "Don't stop me now."

I ejaculated in her mouth. She seemed to like it. It was a first time for her.

She stayed for a few days. The next time we had sex with her on top, she would move her upper body side to side with her nipples rubbing my chest.

What happened to the too sensitive nipples, I wondered? I reached up and grabbed a tit going by, held it in one hand while with the index finger of the other hand, wetted with spit, I rubbed hard on a nipple. After a few minutes, I changed hands and fingers. But this time I noticed she had stopped the body movement, obviously because she liked the wet finger on the nipples better than rubbing them against my chest.

* * *

PWS had a picnic at the local park. Must have been at least six hundred people there. I wandered around greeting everyone. Actually I believe I was seeing what the latest female offerings were. That is when I spotted Jane. Not bad looking. About 5 feet 4 inches tall, maybe 130 pounds, 36C. She had a baby about a year old. Unknown to me at the time, several people were watching me. One said, "Watch Kirk. Any minute now, he will pick up the baby." Just then, I picked up the baby.

Jane invited me to lunch the next day at her house. She served a fine meal. After lunch we went into her living room and chatted about nothing. Surprising, she mentioned her x a few times;

but never said anything bad about him.   That is unusual. Maybe the reason was, she had a beautiful house. It was about 3,500 square feet. Beautifully furnished. I guess this was that rare divorced woman that appreciates what her husband left for her.

I thanked her for the meal and said good bye. She seemed surprised at my announcement and followed me out to the car. I got in as she just stood and watched at the passenger side. She wanted something. I did not know what. Maybe she thought I should kiss her good bye. I had not started the engine. I motioned for her to get in. As she got in I reached across and got her by the hand. She moved all the way across tightly against me. Need I say more. I will skip telling about the pre-play. As soon as she got it in her mouth, she said "Come on back in the house. I am not going to do this out here.

Buck and Bryan both asked me the next day how I made out with Jane. Bryan had already had a blow Job from Jane. Len had had one also and recommend her to Brian.

The next time I saw Jane I asked if she ever had sex the other way, I.E., in the vagina. She said it had been a long time. I also asked if she ever climaxed. She said once in a while. I put it in her vagina and ejaculated.

Buck phoned a couple of days later, asking, "Did you get it in Jane's pussy?"

Turns out, I was a hero. She had passed her mouth around quite a bit; But, I was the only one that put it where it belonged.

She phoned me to say she had been to her doctor. She has pills for me to take. She has a yeast infection in her vagina.

CHAPTER 17

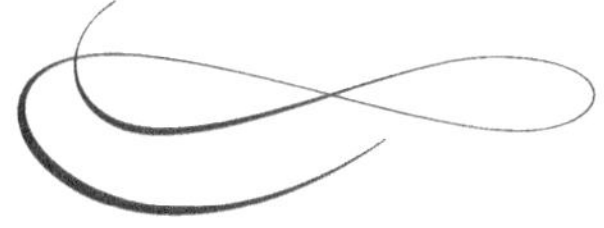

Len Fredricks phoned to tell me he was sick. I already knew that he was sick in more ways than one. He regularly attended PWS activities illegally. He had never been married, and had no children. PWS requires both. I previously mentioned his teen aged girl that he had married, and had sex with her. They could not get her into the United States. He complained because women had changed. He enjoyed the change but hated women for it.

The reason for his phone call was to tell me that one of the women from PWS had been caring for him, "And just like all the rest of the sluts she wants to get laid and I am too tired to accommodate her so I thought of you."

"Len will you ever get it through your thick head these women are not sluts. They are ladies that happen to have normal, uninhibited sexual motivation. Give me her number. I will phone her, ascertain how much you have hurt her, and try to make her feel better. If we both want sex. We will have it. If one of us does not want it. We will find something else to do."

I phoned Mary. We spoke for a few minutes. Then I invited her up. I had not realized it was 4:30. She suggested she would bring a salad. I contributed something.

When she arrived, I quickly realized how beautiful she was. However she was a bit older than most of my friends. She was about my age. We ate then retired to the living room. We sat on opposite side of the room.

As we got to chatting, she told me that she had half a belly button, She had had surgery in Israel and they took the other half. Also she said that after her surgery she was told to wait three months before having sexual relations.

I asked, "when did you have the surgery?"

She didn't answer quickly. She stared at me for the longest time, then said "Three months ago."

She fell on her knees in front of me, and started rubbing my leg. I unzipped my pants and she proceeded to suck until I finished in her mouth. I never got to see that half-belly-button. I wondered what stomach surgery had to do with her using her mouth.

She phoned the next night, inviting me to come to her house to go skinny dipping with her and her two daughters, ages 17 and 15. (*Skinny Dipping is swimming nude*) I made an excuse and never saw Mary again.

* * *

I was getting tired of the kind of life I have had since my divorce from Bonnie. Sex is wonderful. It feels good. Prior to the birth control pill it took some challenge. Condoms and diaphragms and coils required a different frame of mind. One had to be in a proper location to get them. One had to be admitting intention to become involved in a sexual relation.

With the pill the consideration is one is taking it every day so one should be getting some use out of it. If one is out on a date and the necking gets hot, one does not have to go get something before any sexual encounter.

Angela came to my house for the week end. I invited her to attend one of my group discussions. The subject was, *Is it ever right to have sex outside of marriage?* Friday night a group of about 60 gathered in Woodland Hills.

I warned her that some of the participants may seem a little strange to her.

* * *

"Good evening and welcome to PWS group discussion. Our subject for tonight, "Is it ever right to have sex outside of marriage?" My name is Kirk Donaldson. I will be your moderator. Please address all statements to the chair. We will have no cross talk. Don't ask a questions of another person.

What you believe is important is what we want to hear. To start, can anyone give us one reason to justify sexual relationship out side of marriage? Raise your hand if you wish to talk.

About six hands went up. One woman said that in case of where one spouse is physically handicapped the other should be free to have sex outside. A man suggested that he thought it would be ok if like his ex-wife she was cold, she considered sex to be only to have children. My son it 15 years old, and it has been that many years since I had sex with her. I had a neighbor woman who felt sorry for me.

She was having the same problem with her husband. So we got together two or three time a week. It didn't hurt anyone.

Most of the men appeared to be looking at the beautiful blond sitting near me. "Before we go any further, I want to introduce Angela. Will you stand up Angela. Angela and I will be traveling to Israel next month. While we are there, we will become husband and wife. I have moderated many discussions for you. This is the last."

"We have about 15 minutes left. I am going to give you a test. Please give the most honest answer that you can. Take one and pass the balance on."

"As soon as you have finished with the test, please drop it into this basket and help yourself to refreshments. We will count each paper and post the results on the blackboard that we brought in especially for that purpose."

Following is the result;

"On Saturday night witch would you prefer go to;
A religious service 8   PWS party 21   Play volley ball 20

Would you rather;
Have sexual relations 37 Go fishing 14 Watch TV 3

Would you rather;
Have sex on a dirty concrete floor 17   Sit alone on clean chair 31

Would you rather;
Have two sex partners in bed   12   Have one sex partner in bed 36

Do you believe sex outside of marriage is;
OK for those who have never been married. 9
OK for those who have been married.   43"

* * *

Back at my house;

I asked Angela, "How much time can you get off work?"

"I have thought about that. If it is alright with you, I would like to give notice Monday to terminate my employment in two weeks."

"How are you going to support us?"

"Ever hear of living on love?"

"That sounds like a winner to me. Let's live on love."

"I will start looking for a church that is planning a trip to Israel two weeks or so from now. Is that OK?"

It was four weeks until the next trip, and it was with a church in Scranton, PA. So we decided to drive To New York and meet them at Kennedy Airport.

We spent a week driving from Los Angeles to New York. Before each meal, we said grace. We took turns praying at bed time. Sometimes it seemed strange, all of this sincere prayer from two people who were living in violation of god's laws. I thought about *EXODUS, CHAPTER 20, The Ten Commandments. Verse 14, "You shall not commit adultery".* to the best of my knowledge the bible does not specify which of the commandments is more or less important than the others.

CHAPTER 18

We arrived at El Al Airlines, at New York's Kennedy airport where we met our group. We were surprised at how strict security was. We were told to not leave our luggage unattended or it would be thrown into the street.

We boarded the Boeing 747 and prior to take off the leader led our group in prayer.

Landing in Israel, we collected our luggage and boarded a waiting bus. It took us to Caesarea on the Mediterranean coast. Our room had a bowl of fruit and a note welcoming us to Israel. I believed everyone in our group knew that Angela and I were in

Israel to get married. No one seem to wonder why we did not have separate rooms until the wedding.

The next morning after breakfast, we started our guided tour. This was a pile of beach sand until some children playing found rock just a little below the surface. Excavations in the 1950s and 1960s exposed the remains of a Roman city and a Crusader city. The Roman city was walled and was the largest harbor on the east coast of the Mediterranean sea.

In the year 6 CE it became headquarters for the Roman procurators of Provincial Judaea. During excavation, a stone was found with an inscription mentioning Pontius Pilate, Procurator of Judea. I know the Bible fairly well, and to my knowledge, Pilate is mentioned nowhere except in the New Testament when he was summand from Caesarea to try Jesus.

Caesarea is important to Christian history. Cornelius, the first Roman to accept Christ, was baptized here. I do not believe any water was used for this baptism. This may seem strange to some. When John was baptizing in the river, he said, "I baptize you with water. But after me will come one who will baptize you with the Holy Spirit (Mt 3-11)." From here Paul started his journey in the Eastern Mediterranean, and here he was arrested and sent to Rome for trial.

The aqueduct was amazing in that the engineering skill that went into it was what we believed was far ahead of its time. It was a gradual slope from Carmel Mountain.

Theologian Origen who founded a Christian academy had 30,000 manuscripts in the Caesarea library in the fourth century, theologian Eusbius, composed a monumental written history on the beginning of Christianity in the Holy Land.

Christians, Jews, and Samaritans had many houses of worship here.

In the middle of a large hall is a quote from Paul's letter to the Romans (13.3). One wall was decorated with paintings of Jesus and the twelve apostles

In the year 1101 a green glass vessel was found here, and was believed to be the goblet that Jesus drank from at the Last Supper. It is now in the Church of San Lorenzo in Genoa, Italia.

Angela and I agreed that Caesarea was a great surprise to us. It is open to the public and we certainly recommend it to all Christians. I told Angela, "This is only the beginning." We were so thrilled, almost numbed by what we had seen and heard that day that after dinner we bathed, watched a little television and went to sleep after one little kiss.

One thing we saw that surprised us was an active oil well. This was not mentioned in the Bible.

* * *

The next morning after breakfast we loaded our bus that took us to Masada. Masada is flat top portion of a mountain overlooking the Dead Sea. The Dead Sea is on the lowest dry land on earth. It is called 'Dead Sea' because it has no outlet.

The Romans had made camp at the foot of the mountain for two years.

Herod the great built the fortress of Masada between 37 and 31 BCE. During the revolt of the Jews against the Romans in 66 CE, a group of Jews overcome the Roman garrison of Masada. With Masada as their base, they raided the Roman camp for two years.

The last heroic Jewish stand against the Romans in 73 CE took place here. 960 Jewish defenders committed suicide because they would rather be dead than to be enslaved by the Romans. The Zealots (Jews) chose ten men to kill all of the rest. Then they chose one of the ten to kill them and then himself. All died except two women that remained hidden.

Masada was excavated in 1963 to 1965 by hundreds of people from Israel and several foreign countries. I told Angela I would have gladly helped if I had known.

Water was plentiful. It was collected in large rock-hewn reservoirs in the winter from rain water. To maintain coolness inside the rooms the walls were thick layers of stone and plaster. Under a pile of trash, during excavation, was found the remains of a woman, a man and a child along with hundreds of small, bronze scales of the man's armor (probably stolen from the Romans).

I reminded Angela that it took the Romans two years to get up there and we made it in just a few minutes. Of course we took the cable car, and we didn't have a bunch of people rolling stones down on us.

Masada has a storehouse, a small bath house, a large bath house, a western palace, and a Synagogue. I will try to briefly describe each.

The storehouse has a plastered floor. The roofing was constructed of beams, covered with plaster. During the excavation many jars that were used to store grains, wine, oil and other food were found.

The large bath house was surrounded by rooms. The largest of these was elevated with pillars where hot air was blown to heat the room above.

The western palace is the largest building. It is approximately One acre. When Herod lived here it served as his home and office. It was beautifully decorated with mosaic floors and molded panels of stucco on the walls.

The Synagogue is thought to be the best example of early Synagogues. It was part of Herodias construction that was used by the Jews during the revolt. Parts of two scrolls that were found contain parts of Deuteronomy and Ezekiel.

One day was not really enough time to see Masada. Angela suggested that someday maybe we could arrange to stay at the kibbutz by the Dead Sea and visit Masada every day.

* * *

We spent the next three nights at a large hotel in Jerusalem.

We had dinner in the very large restaurant at the Hotel. It was still early so we went out to a night club. It is different in Israel. Our group of eight people all sat at the same table. On the table were liter containers of orange juice, grapefruit juice and a juice that I had never seen before. It was citrus, and tasted like a mixture of orange and grapefruit.

As I sat there at this long table, I started thinking. By now I had gone 10 days without alcohol. For me, that is a record. It did not seem to bother me. I believed that having that beautiful body in bed with me every night could be part of the reason. At home in ten nights, I would have had at least two different women in bed with me. Likely three. That made me think, why was I getting married. Because, I would lose Angela if I didn't marry her. I later realized that was a wrong reason to marry. You don't marry someone to make them do something or to keep them from doing something. One should not plan on marriage to change someone. I have very little control over the future. I think of JAMES 4:13-17., "Now listen, you who say,' Today or tomorrow we will go to this or that city, spend a year there, carry on business and make money. ' Why, you do not even know what will happen tomorrow. What is your life? You are a mist that appears for a little while and then vanishes. Instead you ought to say, "If it is the Lord's will, I will live and do this or that."

"Kirk what is the matter. Are you OK?"

"Oh, I am sorry. I was doing some heavy day dreaming."

"You aren't backing out now are you?"

"Not a chance."

The first morning in Jerusalem, we loaded the bus and went to Qumran. This was on a terrace between the steep high mountains and the Judean desert. In caves high up the cliffs is where the scrolls were hidden. In the 1950's and 1960's Moslem boys, while playing, started finding where they had been hidden for over 2000 years. They sold the first, The Isaiah scroll for what they believed was a lot of money. There was dried ink in the ink wells where the scroll writers did their work. The Moslem Sheppard boys believed they could make more money by tearing the scrolls into pieces and selling the pieces.

Back in Jerusalem we met the shop keeper that had been the original purchaser. We saw an urn that the first scrolls had been in.

At the Hebrew University we saw the Isaiah scroll. It was wrapped around a cylindrical surface that was part of a floor to high mechanism that is set to go under grown if a bomb should ever go off. It was constructed in 1964 and is called the 'Shrine of the Book', one of the imposing sights of modern Jerusalem. It would have been about 30 meters in length if it had been unrolled. The scroll was perfectly in agreement with current Bibles except for one small mark that most agree was a slip of the pen. The scrolls were used to update our modern Bibles.

I told Angela, "Only God could have maintained this scroll for two thousand years and had it agree with the current interpretation of the Bible."

We were happy for the cab drivers. The Jewish drivers did the driving on Sunday. Saturday the Moslem took care of it.

It was easy to tell the Jew from the Moslem, most of the time. If they seem to be walking long distances or riding a donkey they are Moslems. The Jews drive cars.

We observed Moslem children about eight to ten years old begging. They said, "No mama, No papa, one shekel." (A shekel is in Israel like a dollar is in the United States) with their hand out. I was reaching in my pocket when our guide touched my arm and said, "No. Don't give them money. Their father is waiting around the corner to take the money." We walked to the corner, and sure enough he was there. Angela said," That gives me mixed feelings. They are poor."

* * *

We went to breakfast in a very nice restaurant on Saturday morning. It was open and serving. One thing missing, **NO COOKING ON THE SATURDAY.** Back at our hotel, our room was on the 62nd floor. We got on the elevator and waited while it stopped at every floor. No work on Saturday. Pushing the button would have been work.

We took a day trip to Bethlehem where we saw the place where Jesus was born. It had had a gold ring around the exact location. This ring had been stolen years before but had been replaced to avoid contra version as nations were getting ready to fight. The Church of the Nativity was built over the sight. It is on Moslem land. A Moslem shop keeper gave Angela a pearl covered New Testament. It was like handing a thousand dollar bill to her. She was so excited.

* * *

From Bethlehem we went to Lazarus' home. We stood in the street to look at the home. A strange thing happened. A Moslem woman was standing next to us, holding a baby. Angela displayed her friendly attitude toward the baby. The mother offered the baby to her. Being the friendly type that Angela is she accepted, thinking that this was a temporary thing. When she tried to return the baby to its mother, the mother refused to accept it, saying, "You keep. You keep." Our guide had to get involved. He spoke to the mother in her native language and she took the baby back.

He explained to Angela and me that the woman would likely report the baby kid napped and expect to be paid when it was returned.

* * *

The dome of the rock is one of the newer things to see in Jerusalem. It was built in 687 CE, It is located above the well-known western wall. As we approached the dome I found between two flat stones a shell from an electric machine gun. Normally guns are not permitted in the court yard. However one week before a New York Jew had been there with a gun shooting up the place. Israel Military came in fired a few shots and that is all I could learn about it.

There were a couple of hundred pairs of shoes just outside the entry ways to the dome. Inside people were praying. The dome is sacred to three of the world's great religions, viz. Muslim because it is the spot where Mohammed ascended into Heaven. To the Jews and Christians it is the spot where Abraham endured the ultimate test of his faith by offering to sacrifice his son Isaac.

Primarily there are two places where Jesus was crucified and entombed. One is where the **Church of the Holy Sepulcher** was built. This is believed by mostly Roman Catholics. This sight was a vacant pit outside the city walls in the first century AD.

The **garden tomb** is believed by most non-Catholics to be the place. In 1884 General Gordon of the British Army discovered a garden tomb one block from the old city wall. There he noted the rock formations on the hillside above the tomb were shaped like a skull (Golgotha), John 19:17. The stone, shaped like a wheel, about six feet in diameter was rolled back exposing the tomb. Angela commented that she did not care which of the two places was correct, the important thing is that the tomb was empty.

The walk to the Holy Sepulcher was interesting in that it took us thru the narrow walkways of the city where the merchants displayed their goods.

To the Jewish people the Wailing Wall is the most sacred place for prayer. Prayers can be said aloud or in writing. Written prayers were rolled and placed in the cracks between rocks on the wall. The women and men were separated at the wall. As seem to be the custom in all Israel, everyone was welcomed to use the wall. One man asked if I would like to sell my straw hat while we were standing there.

Next we went to Cana in Galilee where Jesus had turned the water into wine. There we were married in a church that was Catholic. A Baptist and a Lutheran married in a Catholic church in a Moslem town in the Jewish state of Israel.

From there we traveled to a beautiful hotel in Tiberius, It was Canadian owned. I did not know how; but many people there knew that we had just gotten married. They wished us long life and happiness in Hebrew. The hotel management gave us a bottle of wine. I still have that bottle, unopened. The pastor told us we could sleep in the same room now that we are married. I think that was so kind of joke. We observed the Arab women show up for work with their long bladed knives. They would spend the day cleaning fish. The Arab men seem to spend the days playing some kind of game at tables. Excavation along the shore discovered coins with a picture of Jesus on one side and "Jesus the messiah king of kings" on the other side.

The whole gang left the hotel after lunch. We walked the short distance to the Sea of Galilee. Angela and I were invited to sit in a row boat that was about 20 feet long.

All of the other members of our group got on a ship that was about one hundred feet long. A rope was attached to the front of our boat and the rear of the larger boat. They towed us out to the middle of the lake where they cut us loose. This was the symbol of a Jewish tradition, cutting the bride and groom from all others.

We could look up at the Golan Heights. The Syrians use to lay up there with riffles and shoot the Israel farmers below. No more, since the six day war when Israel took control of the Ha Golan.

On our way from Tiberius back toward Jerusalem we stopped at a church on a hill above the road. It was built a little before world war two, and paid for by Mussolini. Molded into the walls were both early Jewish and Roman symbols. Even molded into the wall was a picture of the much talked about Ark of the Covenant. When we got to our new hotel, Angela and I looked up the Ark in our Bibles. During Moses forty day stay on the Mount Sinai God instructed him to build the Ark (Ex 19:20; 24:18). It was to be made of shittim wood to house the Tablets of stone. Moses instructed Bezalel and Oholiab to build it (Ex 31).

CHAPTER 19

Angela moved out of her apartment and into the house. The children were both home. We felt like a normal family. Angela had terminated her job and was doing an excellent job of cooking, cleaning and taking care of the children.

One of the first nights that we were home she was preparing spaghetti. I came home with a bottle of wine. Angela turned it down. I drank it by myself. The worst part of it was, I drank the whole bottle. She never said a word; But, Sure gave me some strange looks. When we got in bed she turned her back on me. I asked, "What is wrong Sweetheart?"

"It is the wine on your breath. I don't like it."

"Oh I am sorry. I just thought it would go well with the spaghetti."

Later when doing yard work, I had a six pack of large cans of beer (three quarts) I worked and drank and Angela just looked at me a few times. I got into the car and drove to the market. Bought a half pint of whiskey. Parked a block away from home and drank the whole thing. Consuming alcohol went on. Angela caught me sober one morning and told me, " Kirk, I did not know before I married you that you drank alcohol. I don't want our marriage to terminate. However, I must tell you I will not tolerate your drinking. You must choose between me and the bottle. Is that clear?"

"I don't drink that much sweet heart."

"Remember what I said. Me or the bottle."

I stopped drinking for several days. She went back to being her loving self.

I was working a job locally. That was rare in my business. One day when I had had a really rough day at work, I stopped at a bar on the way home. That was unusual for me. Through all of my years of drinking, I did it almost exclusively at home. When I used to go to parties, dinners and meetings associated with the church, I would never have a drink there. I would wait until I got home then get drunk. Now I can't do that anymore because I have a tee-totaler at home. I still believed that I could stop drinking any time. The bar was loaded with some good looking girls. I was not interested in getting involved with any of them, but I thought I would be more accepted without the wedding ring. So I took it off and put it in my pocket. I sat down at a small table.

A sharp looking female asked, "Would you like some company?"

The light was rather dim. I looked closely and finally said, "Yes Ivy."

"Kirk Donaldson. How the hell are you?"

"Fine. I haven't seen you for a few years."

"I am still around. By the way, what ever happened to that bitch that was cutting in on me that night at the party?"

"I don't know. I took her home and never saw her again. Do you still live the same place?"

"Still do. Do you want to stop bye?"

"For a little while."

We took our separate cars and met at her apartment.

I was waiting at the door when she got there. She reached around me to unlock the door. I put both arms around her and held her tightly.

"Are you in a hurry?"

"Yes. It has been a long time."

We went in. I took off all of my cloths and laid down on the king sized bed. She came in and gave me the same treatment as before. In her mouth. Suck a little. Pull it out. Scream and yell. Over and over again.

I finally made it home at about one AM. Angela was sitting in the living room waiting.

"What is the excuse this time Kirk?" How much did you have to drink?"

"Wait a minute. Don't sentence me until I get a fair trial."

"I am waiting."

"I am very tired. Can we talk about this in the morning?"

"No. We will talk about it right now."

"All right. I had a very hard day at work. Worked late. Stopped at a restaurant. Had one drink. Got in the car. I thought about calling you. I went to sleep for about an hour. Awakened and drove home."

"Kirk. I have a suggestion. Let us go to a counselor. See if we can work out this recurring problem. OK?"

"OK."

We saw the counselor four times. He suggested that Angela try to be more tolerant of my drinking, and that I cut way back on my drinking. We tried. We both really tried. Sex was not the same as before we were married. She didn't like my Lutheran church. We went to her Baptist church. This incompatibility was affecting my work. The children were away at school.

On night I started drinking beer, then wine, then whiskey. I got so drunk that I didn't know what was going on. Then the police show up. One stayed with me and one with Angela in another room. After a while the policeman that had been talking to Angela came in the room where I was waiting and said to me, "You are under arrest."

"For what I asked?"

"For your truculent behavior toward your wife.

From the jail, I phoned a close friend to bail me out.

I talked to an attorney friend who suggested I see psychiatrists, and then make an appointment with the deputy district attorney. If you can get your wife to go with you that would help.

The Deputy D A let me off thanks to Angela's testimony that I was not a habitual problem. We already had one appointment with the psychiatrist before going to the D A. The psychiatrist made six more appointments for me, one each Tuesday. I couldn't understand why he wanted to see me alone. Angels was the complaining one.

I got drunk again. She moved out and in with a girlfriend. I guessed where she was and I drove there. I had not been drinking. The girl friend was not home. We had sex.

A few nights later Angela showed up just when I got home from work. I had not had a chance to start drinking. She was there just to pick up some clothing. We made love. We both enjoyed it.

She came back several times, and I went to her several times. Usually I was drunk.

At my third or fourth visit to the psychiatrist He recommend that I attend an AA meeting, then let him know at our next meeting what I thought about it.

At my next meeting, I told him that it was kind of interesting. Mostly it was sick people who had much more serious drinking problem than I. That day, he hypnotized me. While under I could clearly see that alcohol was involved in every problem that I ever had.

"Mister Donaldson, you are an alcoholic. You are a very sick alcoholic. My prescription for you is that you attend as many AA meetings as you need to stay off the alcohol."

"When did you find out that I was an alcoholic?"

"The first day I met you! I want you to come back next Tuesday and the following Tuesday, and report to me that you have had nothing alcoholic to drink. I mean nothing. Stay away from friends that drink. Make new friends at AA and elsewhere."

I waited three nights before going to see Angela. And when I did, Angela had changed. She had been working for a few weeks. She met some non-drinking guy on the job. Nothing I said made a difference. She said, "Kirk, I will always have some love in my heart for you."

We had a property settlement that included my purchasing a house and a car for her. I only saw her a few times after that.

CHAPTER 20

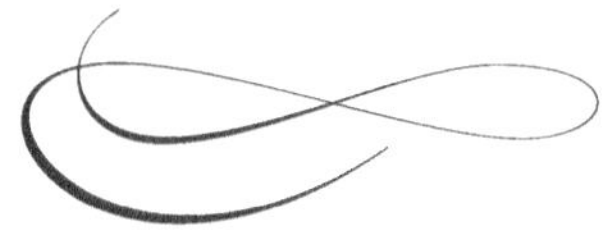

I never had another drink of alcohol. However something was still missing. I learned in AA to pray every night before going to bed and again when rising each morning. I had kept this up for almost two months when one day at work, I had a terrible experience. I was frustrated. I felt like my head was swimming in a circle. My immediate boss took my job away from me and gave it to an engineer that definitely could not handle it. This was when he found that I had spoken to the personal manager about his anti-Mexican attitude. Once I had so many girlfriends. Now I had none. Once Clair Norman had told me that I could charge women with whom I had sex. I felt like I was going to pass out. I decided, I don't care about all of those things I had heard in AA, I am leaving work, going to a liquor store, getting a bottle, and going home and getting drunk.

To this day, I can remember getting in my car. The next thing I can remember, I was home talking to my AA sponsor on the telephone. I know that it was the daily prayer that caused this. The Lord carried me from work to home.

I started back to church regularly. I thank God for my sobriety. I lost interest in seeing how many women could get me in bed. Studying the Bible and teaching it to others was my biggest ambition.

Life is good for me now. My children don't speak to me. My first wife died from cancer. She had been married six times. I was Chairman of the Board of Trustees of my church.

One blessed Sunday morning as I was walking out of church she was standing there about 20 feet from the entrance. At first, I could not believe my eyes. It was a gift from God. I held out both arms as I walked toward her. She did the same. Many people applauded as we got to hold each other tightly.

We now live in a little track house in Prescott, Arizona. We have been happily married for 30 years.